John Baldasare

Knowing Affliction
and Doing Recovery

How to overcome Addictions,
Mental Illness, and PTSD with

The Dayton Model

Books from Higher Ground

Books from Higher Ground
Springfield, Ohio.
http://www.booksfromhigherground.blogspot.com/

Printed in the United States of America 2016

John Baldasare

Knowing Affliction and Doing Recovery

How to overcome Addictions, Mental Illness, and PTSD with

The Dayton Model

Dedication

To the thousands of people I have had the privilege to know over the years that have accessed long-term recovery from addiction, mental illness, and/or PTSD.

Thank you for the education.

This symbol represents The "Big Five" Values of Recovery.

Introduction

What I learned about addiction, mental illness, and PTSD while attending undergrad and graduate studies was minimal. What I learned before then, in my family-of-origin experience, was that these afflictions were moral or will-power related. There was a great deal of judgment and negative emotion in response to behaviors of family members suffering these afflictions. The best, most accurate learning experience for me occurred on the job, where I became an astute observer of the nature of these devastating human conditions, and the process of recovery. I took notes. This written account is the result of that up-close, real life observation.

My first professional job upon graduating college in early 1973 was at a regional state-operated mental institution housing over 2000 people. It had all the appearances of a warehouse for humans and my altruistic self considered it woefully inadequate and downright deplorable. I lasted about six months before taking a job at a county-run detox center.

Our 20 bed open-ward facility was chaotic and usually filled with late-stage alcohol addicts, mostly from the streets, dropped off by police or somehow finding their way to this "station of the lost." I felt quite at home and loved the work. We opened the first residential treatment program in our area a few months after my start there. We had high hopes of helping these people access recovery. There were mixed results at best. There were also great lessons learned. This is when I began collecting observational data.

Over the ensuing years, I found my career taking me all over the country, working in leadership positions in my beloved field. The peak of my career was in the early 90's when I was Executive Director at a renowned addictions treatment center in Arizona, Sierra Tucson, a 183 bed facility that catered to the rich and famous. We treated movie stars, rock stars, professional athletes, and other high-profile or wealthy professionals. All along the way I closely observed the process of recovery, noting what it took to access long-term full recovery from this devastating affliction. I also over the years held director level jobs in mental health and trauma focused programs. The perspective I gained over the 40 years in these settings is what I have to share with you, the reader.

On a more personal note, I was fortunate enough to confront my own addiction to alcohol and have been continuously sober since 1977. My history also involves dealing with PTSD and depression and anxiety. The model of recovery that has emerged from my observations has been applied in my own case with the most positive resolution. For that, and all of my professional experience, I am most grateful.

What follows is what I learned from the thousands of individuals who showed me the path to health and peace-of-mind. My hope is that we can unify our approach to these afflictions and bolster our efforts to save lives and enhance the quality of life for those suffering in these very difficult times.

Affliction is defined as "something that causes pain or suffering". The afflictions of Addiction, Mental Illness, and Post Traumatic Stress Disorder cause great pain and suffering for large numbers of individuals, families, and society. We increasingly see people experiencing what seems to be the main scourge our modern era. Millions of lives are negatively impacted in the United States, and many millions more worldwide. Billions of dollars in costs can be attributed to these afflictions each year. Hundreds of thousands American lives are lost to related events such as drug overdoses, accidents, suicides, and fatal diseases related to these disorders. Our treatment systems are overwhelmed and providers have few solutions that truly result in positive outcomes for most entering their systems of care. The pain and suffering are currently at crisis levels and getting worse.

The purpose of this book is to offer a new, possibly breakthrough method for addressing the aforementioned afflictions. The Dayton Model of Recovery is based upon a perspective gained through the gathering of observational data in the author's 40 years of professional experience in treatment programs addressing these disorders. The Dayton Model claims that there are five things that are very important to know about these devastating disorders, and five things an individual needs to do in order to overcome and access long-term recovery.

The Five Things to Know

First:

The afflicted one is truly sick. These are not moral or criminal matters. These are medical disorders based in the brain. A major problem in perception is that brain-based diseases carry a widely held stigma; a belief by the majority of people that these conditions are self-imposed moral failings that do not deserve the care and resources necessary to successfully treat them. Disorders of other organ systems do not have this kind of negative bias. People with heart, stomach, kidney, liver, or any other systems disruption do receive high quality, compassionate care in our hospitals and physician offices. People with brain illnesses are often left with few options and poor treatment. Once we stop judging, we can start helping. Please know that these fellow citizens are indeed sick.

Second:

It is very important to know just how lonely is the afflicted one. The depth of isolation and separation from others is extreme. The negative judgment, rejection, secrets, denial, misunderstanding, and stigma distances the sick individual from others in every case in every way. This painful reality causes further grief and is self-perpetuating. It simply gets worse over time and becomes a major issue in functioning and impacts outcomes. They are lonely due to an inability to successfully connect with others. They feel different and misunderstood. Rejected and neglected. Lonely hurts.

Third:

Know that the afflicted one is unable to make things better. Try as they might, using all the effort and will that they can muster, nothing done under their own power can positively impact the course of their deteriorating condition. They are unable, not so much unwilling as others might surmise. This inability to make things right, or find a lasting fix, is tremendously frustrating and contributes to their downward spiral.

Fourth:

Guilt is present and pervasive. The afflicted individual concludes that they are "doing bad things", behaviors that go against their value system, and they cannot stop doing those things judged as "bad". The compounding guilt leads to the fifth piece of knowledge needed to truly understand these disorders of the brain.

Fifth:

Shame becomes a growing issue and can lead to thoughts of self-destruction. Many suicides, that permanent solution to a temporary problem, are the result of a deep core of shame in these individuals. Shame is beyond guilt in that the self-talk is around "I am a bad person", or "I am deeply and hopelessly flawed", or "I deserve no better fate in life".

These are killer statements and part of the horrible truth within these afflictions. We have an increasing suicide rate in our society as a result, over 45,000 last year in the U.S. So, the addict, the mentally ill, and the trauma survivor are sick, lonely, unable, guilty, and shamed (s.l.u.g.s.). This is a devastating place to be and is a downward pull to an early demise. We need to help these people, not judge them or forsake them.

The Five Things to Do

First:

For an addiction, Sobriety. For mental illness, Stability. For traumatic stress, Safety. These are the starting points for recovery for these disorders. There really is no other way to begin the process of healing. The addict must get abstinent from their problem drug or behavior in order to enter this solution. The mentally ill must be stabilized, usually with appropriate medication, to enter a recovery opportunity. And the person with PTSD must feel safe to start their recovery process.

Second:

Love is the next necessary step for complete recovery. The afflicted one must come to know that they are cared for in a significant and profound way by professional caregivers, family and friends. Prior to entering this process they are far removed from this awareness, due to the guilt, shame, and self-hatred described. Once they feel loved they can begin doing self-love, leading to the ability to love others. The love ingredient is essential and opens the person to the further developmental potential of true healing. Love does heal.

Third:

Unity with others similarly afflicted. This is the joining-up phase of the ongoing journey to health and wholeness. This step allows the person to know that they are not alone. They come to the realization that others understand and accept them in the common ground of these afflictions. And they discover hope, seeing that others are well on their way to full recovery and are willing to share their experience and what they have found that works.

Fourth:

Growth. Doing self-improvement activities such as psychotherapy, working the 12 Steps, having an exercise routine, changing eating habits, reading self-help material, practicing relaxation techniques, and any other activity that can make them better in any way.

Fifth:

Spirituality is the final piece of the full-recovery puzzle. Practicing activities such as prayer, meditation, immersion in nature, reading inspiration material, an attitude of gratitude, a here and now focus, and belief in a power greater than oneself are all part of a spiritual program which brings peace of mind and leads to long-term recovery.

The solution is then Sobriety, Stability, or Safety for addiction, mental illness, or PTSD correspondingly. Followed by Love, Unity, Growth, and Spirituality (S.L.U.G.S.). This is what works. And it works well provided the program is followed with clarity, specificity, and focused activities accordingly.

The first five chapters of this book will provide excerpts from a Facebook page devoted to these "Big Five Recovery Values". The page SLUGSociety has daily postings from which the following are selected. These five chapters are samplings of that page.

Chapter six is for family and friends, chapter seven for treatment providers, and chapter eight is for prevention programs. The single aim of this offering is to enhance our efforts for better outcomes and making a significant positive impact in the lives of those fellow travelers who are lost in their pain and suffering. It would be a great help if we could all get on the same page with our approach to these devastating disorders and their treatment.

Thank you for reading and considering this option.

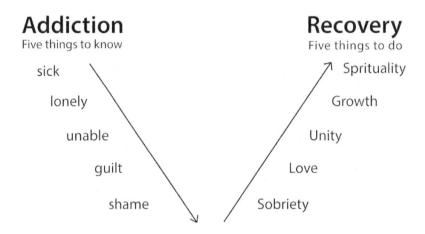

Addiction
Five things to know

sick

lonely

unable

guilt

shame

Recovery
Five things to do

Sprituality

Growth

Unity

Love

Sobriety

Note:

The following five chapters are blog posts taken from Facebook.com/SLUGSociety designed to provide guidance and inspiration to people in the corresponding stage of recovery from addiction, mental illness, and/or traumatic stress. It is suggested that if you are beginning a recovery journey, newly involved in treatment, or seriously contemplating entering a recovery process, that you focus on these brief messages by reading, and rereading, considering the meaning as it may apply to your situation.

Again, these posts are meant to inspire and provide some guidance as you embark on the path to complete recovery. So, focus particularly on the stage of recovery you are in, and consider how this may speak to your individual needs and circumstance. This is the recommended course of action for a new life of health, peace-of-mind, and long-term full recovery.

Chapter 1
Sobriety/Stability/Safety

Recovery value # 1: Sobriety/Safety/Stability

Getting abstinent comes first in the process of recovery from any addiction. If addicted to a drug, medical supervised detox may be necessary.

Whatever the addiction (gambling, sex, a person, etc.) abstaining is the only way to begin the healing journey. This is not an easy step. It may require repeated attempts. Never quit quitting. Your life may very well depend on it.

For trauma survivors, the necessary first step is Safety. If you live in an unsafe environment, where abuse occurs, you will need to leave in order to begin the healing process. For serious mental health issues, Stabilization, often through appropriate prescribed medication, would be the first step toward recovery.

Sobriety/Safety/Stability: The First Recovery Commitment

Beginning the process of recovery can be a daunting task. Knowing that something must change, and then actually making the change, requires courage and action. Getting Sober (Safe for trauma, Stable for mental ills) is often not a onetime deal. We may have to repeatedly begin again, or we may have other addictions that have to be addressed (or new trauma). The point is that these afflictions can be overcome with the knowledge of the path to recovery, and accessing professional resources and supportive networks. Know that recovery is possible. Know that recovery is likely with the right action steps. This is definitely something that can be accomplished.

Sobriety/Safety/Stability Day

Sobriety is the entry point for recovery from addiction. Safety is the entry point for recovery from traumatic stress. Stability is the entry point for recovery from mental illness. Previous to this, it was about being sick, lonely, unable, guilty, and shamed (s.l.u.g.s.). These afflictions have taken the person in totality. The solution is comprehensive. This is all very simple. So you get into the process by getting Sober, Safe, and/or Stable. You get complete and total recovery by following up with Love, Unity, Growth, and Spirituality. This is just what works. I have seen it thousands of times. SLUGS

Sobriety/Safety/Stability Day:

Getting sober is making a statement that enough harm has occurred, enough suffering, enough low quality of life. It is time for a change. Enough is enough. It is time to save this life and enhance it. If drug use or some other behavior is causing problems, it is a problem. It needs to stop (Sobriety). Abstinence contributes to mental clarity. You can now see what is problematic, what needs to change.

If you are in an abusive relationship, get out and to a safe place (Safety). Begin the healing process.

If mental illness is in control, see a Doctor about medication (Stabilization). Recovery starts here.

Sobriety/Safety/Stability:

Addiction, Mental Illness, and PTSD are medical conditions, often referred to as a brain-based diseases. People do not choose these or any other debilitating illness. No one wants to be sick.

In the S.L.U.G.S. Model, the afflicted one is sick, lonely, unable, guilty, and shamed (lower s.l.u.g.s.).

To come up and out of this state of being, one must commit to Sobriety, Safety, and/or Stability. This is the beginning of the healing process. The body gets free of the toxins and the mind gains clarity. Full understanding of the severity of these maladies is possible when sober, stable, and/or safe. Learning all about these conditions and the impact on your life is part of moving toward health. True freedom and an enhanced quality of life begins with your commitment to this first action step.

Sobriety/Safety/Stability: The First Commitment

This is where it all starts. This is also where it stops. Stop the drug use or other addictive behavior, stop being in an unsafe place with hurtful people. Stop the insanity. Getting Sober (or Safe or Stable) provides an opportunity to begin a life changing journey to health and happiness. To commit means to give complete effort and focus toward achieving the goal of freedom from active addiction, or to resolve trauma or psychiatric illness. Help is available. Medical assistance may be needed. A protective environment may be required. Medication may be prescribed.

Nothing easy about any of this. Totally worth it, though.

This is the door to a bigger and brighter life experience. Open the door. Walk through. Welcome to your new life.

Sobriety: Level One Recovery

To be addicted, traumatized, or mentally ill is to be sick, lonely, unable-to-change, guilt-ridden, and shame-filled (s.l.u.g.s.). People do not choose these conditions or this state of being. When one finds that this is reality, then a program of recovery is the necessary course of action. The formula for overcoming starts with a commitment to Sobriety for addiction, Safety for trauma, and/or Stability for mental ills. Medical support is often needed for success in this first phase, especially for drug addiction and mental illness. These are not moral or legal issues. This is a health matter. Make your health matter and get the required help. Make you matter.

Sobriety/Safety/Stability: The First of the "Big Five Values" of Recovery

The first step in the process of recovery is taken out of necessity. The situation has gotten bad enough to require a big change. A problematic life experience that is calling for drastic measures gets our attention. The need in addiction is around abstaining from a drug, a person, or a behavior. The need for traumatic stress is to get to a safe place. The initial need around mental ills is to get stabilized. This beginning point is not easily attained. Get help. This is your chance at recovery. You have to start somewhere, and that place is here.

Sobriety/Safety/Stability: The First Recovery Commitment

Today you can begin a new life with a commitment to Sobriety (Safety for traumatic stress, Stability for mental disorders). This can be the start of an adventuresome life experience, and is reason for real optimism. Millions of people have embarked on this journey of healing and had success in achieving wholeness, a sense of well-being, and peace-of-mind. Do not miss this opportunity. It makes all the difference in terms of a quality life and depth of purpose. Persist, until you succeed. Begin again, if you need. You'll be glad, indeed.

Sobriety/Safety/Stability: SlugStep #1

In some cases, where there is a history of trauma or ongoing psych problems, a need for Sobriety is coupled with a corresponding need for Safety or Stabilization. This means that a dual commitment is required. So, when getting abstinent from a drug, a behavior, or a person, one may have to also get to a safe place or begin a medication regime. The initial assessment of needs must take all three areas into consideration for the best outcomes. Neglecting traumatic stress or psychiatric issues can lead to relapse or keep one stuck in a cycle of failure.

If addicted, it is not possible to find success without first getting sober. For some, staying sober and moving this process forward depends on addressing these other areas.

Sobriety/Safety/Stability Day

This first phase of the recovery process requires that one be honest with oneself. This can be difficult, at best. The element of denial is present in each of these debilitating conditions. The addict may say "I can control this" or "I'll quit tomorrow". The trauma victim may say "It is not that bad" or "They will stop hurting me soon". The mentally disturbed may say "I don't need these meds" or "You are crazy, not me". Some have deeper denial than others. Some seem to be more lost or stuck in their illness. Not everyone makes it up and out of this hell. If you think you have a problem, get help. Get Sober, get to Safety, get Stabilized. Over time, clarity and honesty become reality.

Sobriety/Safety/Stability: Level One Recovery

When one is addicted, traumatized, or mentally ill, action is required in order to begin the process of recovery, or the course of these conditions will continue. Much more pain and suffering will occur and an early death is a likely outcome. This action around getting Sober, Safe, and/or Stable takes courage and determination. To succeed and move through the Five Levels of Recovery, one must remain focused on the end goals of health and peace, and remember to never give up. Courage, determination, focus, and staying power will ultimately bring you home to complete freedom, health, and peace.

Sobriety, Love, Unity, Growth, and Spirituality is Recovery.

Sobriety/Safety/Stability Day:

Sobriety brings opportunity. We stay sober to get the good things in life. Same with Safety for trauma survivors and Stabilization for those with mental illness. This is just the beginning of the path to healing and wholeness.

Leave the hurtful past behind and move forward into the bright new day. Making this commitment is cause for celebration. You fully deserve this chance for peace and happiness. A better life is the promise waiting to be fulfilled.

Sobriety/Safety/Stability

Getting sober is hard enough (safe for trauma, stable for mental illness). Staying sober, safe , or stabilized is harder still. There are forces at work to pull us back into addiction, abuse, or psych distress. One such pull is euphoric recall, where we keep thinking of the good times, forgetting the suffering side. Withdrawal is also a big challenge. Much of this is managed with time. So, being in a place where assistance is available for making it through the tough times in early recovery is very important. 90 days sober, safe, or stable definitely improves perspective and comfort. A year of this new state of mind brings more confidence and a greater chance to go on to full recovery.

Sobriety Day (Safety for trauma, Stability for mental ills):

No one has the goal of becoming addicted, just as no on sets out to be traumatized or mentally ill. When this reality strikes, it is difficult to accept. A struggle ensues around feeling confused and hurt, looking to blame, feeling the shame, wanting to run and hide. Facing these challenges is not easy. We don't choose to get sick, we just know we want to be well. It takes a firm and focused commitment to good programs available, staffed by caring, experienced helpers. They are waiting to do their thing for you. Just show up and begin the healing. It is about a desire for a better life. Once Sober, Safe, and/or Stable, love and peace can arrive. There are good programs available, staffed by caring, experienced helpers. They are waiting to do their thing for you. Just show up.

Sobriety/Safety/Stability: The First Recovery Commitment

Addiction, traumatic stress, and mental illness are all tragic conditions in life that bring suffering and often early death. The down side is extreme. The way up and out is now clear.

First, one must get Sober, Safe, and/or Stable in order to begin a healing process. This simply is where we must start. It can be no other way. To continue in active addiction, a stressful situation, or with mental instability, is to continue on a destructive path.

SLUGS is a constructive, productive path. May you find it now.

Sobriety/Safety/Stability: Commitment One

Getting Sober (or Safe, Stable) is obviously a big challenge for anyone addicted (or traumatized, unstable). This is the basic first step in a lifetime journey of healing. Staying sober is an even bigger challenge. Expect to be tested by people, places, and things that attempt to dissolve your resolve. The concept of one-day-at-a-time helps. We only have to do it for today. If you are in a state of craving or euphoric recall, allow it to pass naturally by staying the course for this day.

You will likely have more clarity after a night of rest. Clarity builds with time. Each day brings an increase in strength. Practice continued commitment. You will be amazed.

Sobriety/Safety/Stability: Recovery Value # 1

Life is a grand creative project. Getting to Sobriety (or Safety for trauma, Stability for mental illness) is the beginning of this great adventure, the entry onto the path of recovery and spiritual growth. However, getting to this point means having had some truly painful and frightening experiences. A price has been paid for this opportunity. Addiction, traumatic stress, and mental instability are serious, life threatening matters. Making this commitment is essential to life and this grand and wonderful process.

Sobriety/Safety/Stability: The First Recovery Commitment

Without a commitment to Sobriety (Safety for trauma, Stability for mental illness), we have no opportunity for recovery. This is the necessary first step in the process of healing. Once this commitment is made, and one is firmly established for some days or weeks, then the other healing factors are workable to sustain the whole process. For example, Love can become a significant promoter of wellness when one is Sober, where it was not at all available when the addiction is active. The same is true of the other essential healing elements of Unity, Growth, and Spirituality. It all starts with the first commitment. Are you ready to begin? Your life may depend on it.

Sobriety/Safety/Stability Day

Getting sober is hard enough (safe for trauma, stable for mental illness). Staying sober, safe, or stabilized is harder still. There are forces at work to pull us back into addiction, abuse, or psych distress. One such pull is euphoric recall, where we keep thinking of the good times, forgetting the suffering side. Withdrawal is also a big challenge. Much of this is managed with time. So, being in a place where assistance is available for making it through the tough times in early recovery is very important. 90 days sober, safe, or stable definitely improves perspective and comfort. A year of this new state of mind brings more confidence and a greater chance to go on to full recovery.

Sobriety/Safety/Stability

In getting Sober (Safe for trauma, Stable for mental ills), you are embarking on a journey toward healing from a devastating condition. Addiction, traumatic stress, and mental illness all have the capacity to take your life from you, and cause much suffering and loss. If you are experiencing harm or life problems due to drug use, attachment to a destructive relationship, or some other behavior, that is a call to you to get abstinent from that drug, person, or activity.

What causes problems is a problem. If you are living in an unsafe environment, get to a safe place. If you are mentally disturbed, seek out medical help.

These actions are life saving. This is the first step. Life is anew, for you.

Sobriety/Safety/Stability: Level One Recovery

This is the beginning of a new life with limitless possibilities. Whereas addiction, trauma, and/or mental illness has brought forth pain and confusion, Sobriety, Safety, and/or Stabilization brings clarity and direction. Now the world begins to open up in ways we could not imagine previously. The miracle of recovery starts here. Make the commitment to enter this process and you will never regret it. Enter the journey of a lifetime.

Sobriety/Safety/Stability Day:

As it happens, the recovery process does not usually have finality about it. There often arises a need for continuation or beginning again, with multiple addictions, a new trauma, or recurrent mental disorder. So, if you find that after recovery from a drug addiction, you are harmfully dependent on a person or activity, the necessary intervention is to re-engage the "Big Five" commitments of recovery. It is time to get Sober once again to begin the process.

For traumatic stress, it is time to get to Safety, a safe place, to begin recovery again. For a new mental disturbance, it is time to get Stabilized. The important thing is to do the recovery thing whenever the need arises. This solution works again and again. Sobriety, Love, Unity, Growth, and Spirituality will bring you home to peace each time. SLUGS!

Sobriety/Safety/Stability: The First Value/Commitment

Safety means immediate freedom from active traumatic stress.

Stability means immediate freedom from active mental disorder.

This is the beginning of a path to lifelong freedom furthered by the other four of the "Big Five" Values of Recovery. Freedom to Love, freedom to Unite, freedom to Grow, freedom to live in the Spirit. Freedom defines recovery. Free to be healthy and happy.

Sobriety/Safety/Stability Day:

It is problems in life that causes us to seek solutions. Addiction, traumatic stress, or mental disorders cause one to be sick, lonely, unable, guilty, and shamed (lower slugs), a state of suffering. To come up and out of this place, to save one's own life, and to emerge into the light of health and peace, a commitment to Sobriety, Safety, or Stabilization is necessary. Sometimes a slip back to the unhealthy place occurs. Commit again. If you slip, get up. Begin again. No failure is final, unless death occurs. As long as you are still breathing, you have a chance at the higher life.

Sobriety/Safety/Stability: Recovery Value One

This whole thing of needing to get Sober (Safe for trauma, Stable for mental ills) starts and ends with saving a life. Your life. The fact is that too many are dying of addiction, PTSD, and mental illness. So many lives have been lost. Young lives in so many cases. The recent surge of heroin overdose deaths is especially disturbing. It is important to not get stuck in the sadness of this reality. There is hope with the process of recovery. The first step is Sobriety, Safety, Stability. May you commit now, today. Begin the journey to healing and wholeness. Nothing matters more.

Sobriety/Safety/Stability: The First Recovery Commitment

When we commit to Sobriety (Safety for trauma, Stability for mental disorders) we are saying that it is time to change it up. The need for a new start in life has become very apparent. The old way is not working anymore. Dependence on a drug, a person, or some harmful behavior, is taking us down. The situation is unsafe, the mind is out of control. Abstinence, a safe place, stabilizing medication, are life saving measures. This commitment requires great effort to fulfill, and sometimes requires professional/medical assistance. Emerge. Engage. Live.

Sobriety/Safety/Stability Day:

We just know one day that change has to come. Pain has a way of getting our attention. If my alcohol or other drug use is hurting me in some way, or hurting those I love, it is time to give abstinence a go. So it is get Sober, do everything to stay that way, and do it again, if necessary.

With trauma, it is get to Safety, stay there, go there again, if necessary. For mental illness, get Stabilized, stay stable, and get it again, if necessary. The point is to take this important first step, stick with it, and do it again if it does not stick.

Never give up. It is worth the effort.

Sobriety/Safety/Stability: Level One Recovery

Sobriety is for addiction recovery. Safety is for traumatic stress recovery. Stability is for mental illness recovery. This is about making a firm commitment to begin a process which leads to freedom, health, connection, and peace of mind. It is a decision to start life anew, to give yourself a chance for true happiness and wholeness. The ongoing suffering, confusion, fear, and aimlessness can now cease. Let it end. Begin again. Today.

Sobriety/Safety/Stability: Recovery Value #1

When one has 90 days of continuous Sobriety (Safety for trauma, Stability for mental disorders), this usually makes for a point of more clarity and confidence. Then the second phase of recovery is more readily available/accessible. How does one accomplish the 90 days marker? Some must enter a medical setting to safely detox from alcohol or other drugs. Others, in less physical distress, are just so fed up with their current state that this option is a must. Then it is a one-day-at-a-time effort, getting support and inspiration from others. Getting started is the most important thing. Get on with this journey. Life will become awesome.

Sobriety/Safety/Stability : The First Recovery Commitment

It is helpful to verbalize your commitment to Sobriety (Safety for trauma, Stability for mental ills). Telling someone close to you your intentions to begin healing is a potent act. If in a treatment setting, tell the whole group that you are committed to begin the process. It is only natural that you will gain their support. Making a statement of intention/commitment solidifies and focuses your efforts. This is the first step in your journey to healing and wholeness. Let the good life ensue. Stay committed and true.

Sobriety/Stability/Safety

Sobriety whole thing of needing to get Sober (Safe for trauma, Stable for mental ills) starts and ends with saving a life. Your life. The fact is that too many are dying of addiction, PTSD, and mental illness. So many lives have been lost. Young lives in so many cases. The recent surge of heroin overdose deaths is especially disturbing. It is important to not get stuck in the sadness of this reality. There is hope with the process of recovery. The first step is Sobriety, Safety, Stability. May you commit now, today. Begin the journey to healing and wholeness. Nothing matters more.

Sobriety/Safety/Stability: Level One Recovery

This is the beginning of a new life with limitless possibilities. Whereas addiction, trauma, and/or mental illness has brought forth pain and confusion, Sobriety, Safety, and/or Stabilization brings clarity and direction. Now the world begins to open up in ways we could not imagine previously. The miracle of recovery starts here. Make the commitment to enter this process and you will never regret it. Enter the journey of a lifetime.

Sobriety/Safety/Stability Day:

Sobriety brings opportunity. We stay sober to get the good things in life. Same with Safety for trauma survivors and Stabilization for those with mental illness. This is just the beginning of the path to healing and wholeness.

Leave the hurtful past behind and move forward into the bright new day. Making this commitment is cause for celebration. You fully deserve this chance for peace and happiness. A better life is the promise waiting to be fulfilled.

Sobriety/Safety/Stability: SlugStep #1

In some cases, where there is a history of trauma or ongoing psych problems, a need for Sobriety is coupled with a corresponding need for Safety or Stabilization. This means that a dual commitment is required. So, when getting abstinent from a drug, a behavior, or a person, one may have to also get to a safe place or begin a medication regime. The initial assessment of needs must take all three areas into consideration for the best outcomes. Neglecting traumatic stress or psychiatric issues can lead to relapse or keep one stuck in a cycle of failure.

If addicted, it is not possible to find success without first getting sober. For some, staying sober and moving this process forward depends on addressing these other areas.

Sobriety/Safety/Stability: The First Commitment

This is where it all starts. This is also where it stops. Stop the drug use or other addictive behavior, stop being in an unsafe place with hurtful people, stop the insanity. Getting Sober (or Safe or Stable) provides an opportunity to begin a life changing journey to health and happiness.

To commit means to give complete effort and focus toward achieving the goal of freedom from active addiction, or to resolve trauma or psychiatric illness. Help is available. Medical assistance may be needed. A protective environment may be required. Medication may be prescribed.

Nothing easy about any of this. Totally worth it, though. This is the door to a bigger and brighter life experience. Open the door. Walk through. Welcome to your new life.

Sobriety/Safety/Stability: The first of the "Big Five" for Recovery

One arrives at the doorway to recovery having experienced the sickness, loneliness, unableness, guilt, and shame (lower slugstate) that is the hallmark of addiction, traumatic stress, and/or mental illness. It is upward and onward from here. By following this simple and clear path, one moves quite assuredly from illness to health, from sorrow to joy, from despair to hope, from problem to solution. The path? Sobriety, Love, Unity, Growth, and Spirituality. In that order.

Powerful stuff. The truth.

Sobriety/Safety/Stability: The Number One Recovery Value

At the starting point of this new life experience, we leave behind addiction, traumatic stress, and/or mental illness by getting Sober, Safe, and/or Stable. Thus begins the recovery process.

There is no other place to launch from. So, with the help of medical professionals, this life-saving, life-enhancing project can be initiated. This is cause for celebration. A great opportunity for expansion and actualization has been provided. Life gets going in the right and best direction now. The path to full recovery is clearly revealed. Sobriety, Love, Unity, Growth, and Spirituality (SLUGS). Begin a new life.

Sobriety/Safety/Stability: The First Recovery Commitment

Sobriety allows entry to the addiction recovery process. Safety is the access point for trauma resolution. Stabilization brings the opportunity for recovery from mental illness. These starting places are the first phase of a five step process that delivers full recovery. An important part of remaining Sober, Safe, and/or Stable involves learning about these afflictions. The more we know about the nature and course of addiction, traumatic stress, and/or mental illness the better. Knowledge gives power. Know thyself and thy illness.

Sobriety/Safety/Stability Day:

In the SLUGS Model of treatment for addictions, the first phase of care is directed by medical professionals. Detox can be complicated and needs close monitoring. For trauma and mental illness, medications may also be prescribed in Level One Care. Level Two Care (Love) is provided primarily by counselors, Level Three (Unity) is peer driven, Level Four (Growth) is often provided by psychotherapists, and Level Five (Spirituality) is by those of Higher Consciousness. This approach involves specialists and disciplines that insure comprehensive recovery in a systematic way. It works.

Sobriety/Safety/Stability: Recovery Initiated

To enter the process of recovery from addiction, traumatic stress, and/or mental disorders, one must get Sober, Safe, and/or Stable. There is no other point of initiation. Stuck in these states of illness and suffering, this first step is difficult and scary. We are going into an area that is unfamiliar. Know that this new beginning offers the promise of health, freedom, and peace. Once we are in this process, some momentum can take hold and we basically launch into a new lifestyle, a new life. This is nothing short of transformation, ascending to Higher Consciousness.

This is a big deal. Go for it.

Sobriety/Safety/Stability: The First of the "Big Five Values" of Recovery

The first step in the process of recovery is taken out of necessity. The situation has gotten bad enough to require a big change. A problematic life experience that is calling for drastic measures gets our attention. The need in addiction is around abstaining from a drug, a person, or a behavior. The need for traumatic stress is to get to a safe place. The initial need around mental ills is to get stabilized. This beginning point is not easily attained. Get help. This is your chance at recovery. You have to start somewhere, and that place is here.

Sobriety Day, Safety Day, Stability Day

Whether we are dealing with addiction, traumatic stress, and/or mental disorders, we must take action in order to begin the process of recovery. This stuff does not resolve without our participation. The starting point is Sobriety for addiction recovery, Safety for trauma resolution, and Stabilization for mental ills. Once Sober, Safe, and/or Stable, the miracle of full recovery begins to manifest. It is a wondrous experience to behold. Be bold. Access recovery today.

Sobriety/Safety/Stability

The addict needs Sobriety. The trauma survivor needs Safety. The mentally ill needs Stabilization. This is where recovery starts. The process begins. Often professional oversight is required in order to achieve this initial aspect. Good help is available. Then the glorious recovery process can unfold with Love, Unity, Growth, and Spirituality providing the remaining pieces of the solution.

Sobriety/Safety/Stability: Recovery Value One

In order to overcome addiction, traumatic stress, and/or mental illness one has to start somewhere. So recovery, the overcoming and rising up, starts with Sobriety, Safety, and/or Stability correspondingly.

Recovery as a process involves five phases. This first phase is the foundation for the rest, the grounding. After this part is established, the further process of Love, Unity, Growth, and Spirituality can unfold and deliver one to full recovery and a new life experience.

Sobriety Day (Safety for trauma, Stability for mental ills)

We do this thing called recovery initially because we have to. Our life depends on it. The quality of our life depends upon our willingness to take action and get this thing moving toward resolution/recovery. Once we are committed and acting accordingly, we realize that this is not only what we must do, but what we want to do. So, get in the game. Long-term recovery, and a happy, healthy, peaceful life awaits you through this process. It begins with Sobriety/Safety/Stability.

Sobriety/Safety/Stability: The First Recovery Commitment

Making the commitment to enter the realm of recovery from addiction (Sobriety), traumatic stress (Safety), and/or mental illness (Stability), means that we are serious about making a better life for ourselves and our loved ones. Taking this first step provides hope and incentive to continue on a path of superior health and well-being. We want life to work on the highest level. That is why we do this recovery thing.

Chapter 2
Love

Recovery value #2: Love

Accepting and embracing the care and positive regard provided by counselors/therapists/helpers is crucial for recovery. It is in their nature to be compassionate and empathic. All people want love. All addicts need love. Let it be. Commit to the process.

Self care is part of this phase of recovery. Beginning to love and accept who you are allows this process to continue.

Great benefit is derived from caring for others. Often an opportunity to provide encouragement and support to others will arise and a good feeling comes from doing the loving thing.

Let the love light shine on you and help you to heal.

Love Day:

Starting a recovery process with a heavy load of guilt, shame, and self-hatred makes love a distinct need. Opening to loving kindness provided by counselors and concerned friends and family, is where this begins. Open your heart to the people in your life who really care. You know who they are. They will walk with you to the healing place. They will love you until you can love yourself.

"All you need is love.....and Sobriety, Unity, Growth, and Spirituality".

Love:

When recovering from addiction, trauma, or mental illness by way of the S.L.U.G.S. Model, love promotes healing once one is Sober, Safe, and/or Stable. An openness occurs, an opportunity to allow for the sweet goodness available from the truly caring helpers. A smile, a hug, a kind word of encouragement, all serve to nudge one forward on the path. There are healers in our midst who have big hearts bursting with loving energy. They simply must share their wealth with those in need. Let them in. Open your heart to their offering. Everybody wins. It is a beautiful thing.
Love: The Second Commitment

We all want and need love. Love is soothing. Love is refreshing. Love motivates. Love is a big deal. Wallow in love. Swim in it. Breathe it in. Study love. Once you have a clear mind (Sobriety), you can have an open heart (Love).

Ask: Who loves you? Who do you love? Who really cares? Embrace and express.

This is a high priority in recovery. It is yours for the taking. Believe in Love. Look for opportunities to do the loving thing and allow others to do for you. Explore self love. Healing is propelled by love.

Love: SlugStep #2

Caring, positive regard, warmth, acceptance, hugs, smiles, helpfulness, hopefulness, guidance, protection, forgiveness, peace, kindness, friendship, being heard, a pat on the back, encouragement, laughter, togetherness, equality, mutuality.

These are all love related, love connected. People who consistently value and behave in these ways are ahead of the game. Be around the gentle, caring folks and strive to be that person. Do these things for yourself. Move this recovery thing along in this way. Do love, be love.

Love Day:

Addiction is marked by the absence of love and the presence of fear. Remove the fear and love emerges. The light of love replaces the darkness of fear. There are caring, loving humans all around who give freely. Avail yourself of their kindness.

To forgive is to love. To forgive ourselves is to love ourselves.

Love: Level Two Recovery

In Level Two one only needs to commit to finding love, giving love, being love. This is a very healing aspect of the process. While in a treatment program, loving kindness and caring is readily available from the empathic staff members. Most of these people have much to offer in this regard. Soak it up. Again, it is "they loved me until I could love myself". You also need to identify the family members and friends who truly love you, and then stay close to them. Relax into the sweet balm of love.

Love Day

When active in addiction, traumatized, or mentally unstable, love is somehow absent, unavailable even. Too much fear.

Once sober, safe, and/or stable, love emerges to soothe and heal. When the negative, scary stuff dissipates, we can relax into the warmth and positive regard being offered by caregivers, family, and friends. Over time, as one gathers a storehouse of love, the giving of love, to oneself and others, brings even greater benefit and reward. Love is powerful. Love endures. Love rules.

Love: Recovery Value # 2

Everyone desires that loving feeling. We all want to feel protected and valued and supported and accepted as we are. It is only natural. When in active addiction, traumatic stress, or mental instability, the absence of love is due to being wholly distracted and in a survival mode. Getting to Level 2 in this process allows for the free flow of love and caring. People generally want to be kind. So, staying sober, safe, and stable brings out the goodness. Let love spill over like beautiful molten lava.

Love Day:

Love is the greatest healing power on earth. That is why in this recovery model, love follows the initial event of getting Sober, Safe, and/or Stable. A crucial factor in this regard is the environment in which we choose to place ourselves. A treatment center must have a loving, deeply caring staff in order to do their jobs right. If living at home while engaged in a recovery program, it is essential that the environment is non-toxic and highly supportive and loving. Be around people who believe in you and truly want the best outcome for you. Winners are surrounded by loving people. Consciously seek love and protection.

Love: Commitment Two

If you were continuously and consistently loved and nurtured as a child, you will likely have no trouble with self-love. If you were abused, betrayed, or abandoned in some way, this whole love thing is elusive and challenging. The important thing today is to place you in a safe, nurturing environment around people who can and do consistently offer positive regard and caring. Sometimes we find what we need in our immediate family. Some have to search for the loving people. Love requires practice and a commitment to self-care and forgiveness. It just takes time and effort to get where we are going.

Love Day:

As love enters, fear vanishes. An important part of the recovery process involves allowing the love feeling to enter our hearts and minds. That means availing ourselves to those who are willing and able to provide the supportive, nurturing, healing positive regard and unconditional love. Hard to find? Treatment programs and recovery support groups have these people in abundance. As the fear leaves, then self-love has more room to enter. As love grows, we are inclined and able to reach out in a loving manner to all.

Love: The Second Value/Commitment

When love is presented to one beginning a recovery process, it is initially met with some resistance. One may ask "Am I deserving?", "Do they really care about me?", "Will this last?"

Just be open. Just accept the caring and encouragement. It will serve to heal the wounds of the past and bring you to a place of self-acceptance and positivity. It just takes time. Soak it up. Wallow in it. Allow love to wash over you and soothe you.

Love Day:

The pain of active addiction, traumatic stress, and/or mental distress leaves one feeling raw and vulnerable. In order to heal from the lingering damage of these conditions a compassionate, kind, and loving response from caregivers, friends, and family certainly is helpful and necessary. This is a time when you find out who really stands in your corner and will be there for you. You find out who really has the caring heart. You find out who has your back. It is important to sort this out. Step away from the negative, hurtful types and gravitate toward the light and love.

Love Day:

In early recovery, the openness to caring and love from others is very important. It is also crucial to begin practicing self-love. This entails caring for self by getting adequate rest, nutrition, activity, and release of negative attitudes. We start to believe in ourselves and our ability to overcome addiction, trauma, and mental disorders. We practice affirmations that uplift us. "I will greet this day with love in my heart". "I will persist until I succeed".

Love: Level Two Recovery

There are three parts to this phase of the recovery process.

First, we must allow others to provide care and comfort to our wounded, fearful selves. This soothing experience heals.

Second, we practice self-care, doing comforting and healing action concerned with what we can do for ourselves, self-soothing stuff.

Third, we begin to reach out in a caring manner to others. We realize that giving love and support brings back to us a feeling of worth and purpose. And the love grows and goes, to and fro.

Love: Recovery Value #2

With many years of experience working in treatment centers, the basic needs of those suffering these disorders has become clear. The sense of separation and loneliness is profound. So, presenting compassionate caring, understanding, and acceptance is what helpers know they must do. Your role in this phase of the process is to let the love be, let it flow. The counselors, medical staff, your family and friends, will want to demonstrate their genuine concern. It is time to choose allowing this goodness to wash over you and you then will realize what it means when someone says "you loved me until I could love myself".

Love: The Second Recovery Activity

This Love phase of the recovery process comes in three parts. After getting Sober, Safe, and/or Stable, one avails oneself to the care and loving kindness of others. This often takes place in a treatment program setting and is provided by counselors and family members. Part two is learning to Love oneself. This is a big challenge in that addiction, trauma, and mental illness all contribute to self-hatred. So, with practice and some time in recovery, a person can become more self-love oriented and overcome the negative perceptions of self. The third part is around providing Love to others. This brings it full circle and creates a situation of perpetuating Goodness and Light.

Love Day:

Once a person becomes Sober, Safe, and/or Stable, an openness to the Love experience occurs naturally. When stuck in the illness states, the sense of separation and the self-loathing keeps Love out, creating distance, unavailability. So, at Level Two of the recovery process, a whole new world of possibility emerges. We can accept Love/Caring from others, we can begin to Love ourselves, and we feel a pull to express more Love for others. The movement toward healing is thereby accelerated. Love propels one to new heights and a great sense of relief. Hope bubbles up.

Love: The Second Recovery Commitment

To commit to Love involves allowing helping professionals to give support, encouragement, soothing words, kindness, acceptance, and positive regard. It is about staying in the environment of care. Too much negativity and hurt has ruled previously. We must make ourselves available for this healing action, the wrapping of self in Love from caregivers, loving family members, and true friends. This commitment pays off with a better sense of self-care and the ability to offer ourselves in a helpful way to others in need

Love Day:

The power of Love is beyond measure. Each of us has a strong pull toward Love, to Love and to be Loved. From our first day of existence this has been true, with receiving Love most necessary early on. The damage from addiction, traumatic stress, and/or mental disorders actually creates a greater need for Love, in order to bring about healing and overcome the deep negativity that is experienced with these conditions. Love from caregivers and family, unconditional self-love, and doing the loving thing are all important. Be open to Love. Be willing to Love. Just Love!

Love: The Second of the "Big Five" for Recovery

This is clearly not about romantic love, that charged-up, sometimes fleeting state that can go so wrong, even leading to addictive, dependent relationships. This is about something deeper and more meaningful. It is about caring for someone's well-being. It is about providing nurturance and emotional support. It is mostly about being there for one in need of recovery from a devastating condition that is life-threatening. This is about compassion and loving-kindness. Love that is true is from the depths of our souls. It expresses the divine impulse of healing energy. Let love be given. Let self-love arise. Give what you can.

Love: Recovery Value #2

The active addict, the trauma victim, and the mentally ill, all feel unlovable. It is just the nature of these conditions. When exposed to the depth of love and caring provided by health professionals, family members, and true friends in the second phase of recovery, the miracle of recovery starts to manifest. As the healing one feels loved and more lovable, the ability to love emerges. The person in recovery realizes that they are capable of extending love to others and back to oneself. This is profound. The impact on the process of recovery is such that one knows without doubt that healing is taking place and a deep hope for ongoing success is present.

Love: Recovery Commitment #2

The wounded soul responds favorably to Love. When a person enters a care environment (hospital, treatment program, etc.) the first order of business is around issues of comfort, trust, support. The need to know fully that caring and kindness is a priority sets the tone for the experience. One goes into these places with fear, having difficulty trusting and accepting help.
The workers in these settings have dealt with these issues and know the importance of giving the loving response time and again. It starts and ends with Love. "Love is the greatest refreshment in life". - Pablo Picasso

Love Day:

To be addicted, traumatized, or mentally ill, means that one is sick, lonely, unable, guilty, and shamed (lower s.l.u.g.s.). This state is obviously love deprived. We need to feel the warm glow of Love and kindness in order to begin to rise up from this place of desperation. We must choose to be with any and all of the nurturing, empathic people that we can locate. They are to be found in healing places such as treatment centers and clinics, as well as in our families. It is important to choose carefully. Anytime you find yourself with mean or uncaring people, change it up. Get away from the hurters, get with the helpers. It will make all the difference in your recovery opportunity.

Love: The Second Recovery Commitment

The addict, trauma victim, and the mentally ill feel undeserving of Love. Often times it is difficult to love them. The behavior from hurting people is often hurtful to others. How do you overcome the hurt? How do you forgive and actually move on to a place of compassion? The answer is around how you view the disordered person, whether we are referencing ourselves or another. It is important to see that the addict, the trauma victim, and the mentally ill are sick. This behavior is not intentional, nor is it personal. If they, or we, could do better, we would. One is either in their sickness, or in their recovery. Love those suffering these conditions. Love heals.

Love: Level Two Recovery

To helpers, family, and friends of those addicted, traumatized, or mentally ill: Love them. Just pour forth from your heart all the caring and support that you can muster. Yeah, it takes effort sometimes. These folks have behaved in ways that make it more difficult. You may have to go to forgiveness first (remember they are sick). It does not help whatsoever to judge, punish, or criticize. Be compassionate. Know that your response and attitude can foster healing or drive a person toward despair. The person with these conditions needs to know "I am loved", then "I am loving", then "I am Love".

Love Day

Having worked for many years in treatment settings, it became apparent along the way that those with addictions, traumatic stress, and mental disorders responded favorably to loving kindness and positive regard. It was obvious that anyone who could not present this way was not suited to work in these settings. We knew that our staff selection criteria had to start with who could be compassionate and really love our patients without conditions. Some workers had personal issues that got in the way. They had to resolve these or leave. Love is paramount in the early stage of recovery. Once Sober, Safe, and/or Stable, Love works to sustain the process. Love wins.

Love: The Second Recovery Commitment

A person gets to the point in active addiction, traumatic stress, and/or mental illness where they wonder if anyone really cares about them. The amount of self-doubt, rejection, isolation, and fear present in these conditions just takes a toll. In order to overcome this aspect of disorder, one must seek out the caring others. These love-givers are found working in treatment centers and will be there to provide acceptance and understanding to anyone committing to this phase of recovery. Ask yourself: "Who loves me?" "Who will support my recovery efforts?" You may also find these kind and supportive people in your family and friends. You will know who is with you.

Love Day:

Once a person becomes Sober, Safe, and/or Stable, they have become ripe for the experience of Love. Walled off from that opportunity when in the depths of addiction, trauma, or mental illness, now an opening has occurred as a result of the first recovery phase. Available to receive caring and support from caregivers and capable others, another opportunity for Love arises. One can begin to Love and care for oneself. The depths of self-care can now be explored and realized. Caring enough to remain immersed in the process of recovery, and beginning to care about fellow travelers on this road, leads to a more complete healing. Wholeness begins to form. Emergence to Love launches one to greater heights.

Love: The Second Recovery Value

Once Sober, Safe, and/or Stable, the recovering individual needs Love in order to continue on this path to healing and wholeness. It is as if the Love pushes one forward, providing the necessary thrust. Love also gives motivation to continue the journey. It is a reason to remain in the process. "They love me, perhaps I am worth the effort".

Then the Love for self begins to manifest. "They love me, I can love myself". This Love thing inspires more Love. Reaching out and providing support and encouragement to others just feels good. As you get it, you want to give it. It becomes circular. Get it, give it. Give it, get it.

Love Day:

Addiction hurts. Love heals. Traumatic stress hurts. Love heals. Mental illness hurts. Love heals. Love is not the total answer. The other four recovery values are still necessary ingredients in this formula for health and well-being. Following Sobriety, Safety, and/or Stability, the Love we receive corresponds to the Love we feel we deserve. This is a challenge in that we find it difficult to believe we're loved when we feel unlovable. Continue to hang with those who easily provide that deep caring and support. Stay in a formal care system and spend time with loved ones and loving ones. Believe in the power of Love and know that you are fully deserving of Love.

Love: Level Two Recovery

This is how it works. When one commits to recovery and enters a care system, becoming Sober, Safe, and/or Stable, counselors usually become the primary caregivers. Who are these people and what do they want? They are compassionate and knowledgeable professionals who want to see you become whole and healthy. They want to assist your process. They know what is possible and what is likely if you follow the prescribed plan. They will walk with you and give you kindness and honest feedback. These are guides to wellness. Allow this process to unfold. Permit this love and care. These people are in your life providing a life saving purpose.

Love: The Second of the "Big Five Values" of Recovery

Once this recovery process is initiated through the act of getting Sober, Safe, and/or Stable, the next obvious need is around Love.

There remains a wounded person who can definitely use the soothing nature of kindness, caring, and genuine positive regard. Treatment program staff members are built to provide this healing power, and are prepared to do just that. They convey acceptance and understanding. They convey hope and belief in the embattled one. They are willing and able to show the way to full recovery. Being open and available to this Love is crucial. Ultimately, Love heals

Love: The Second Recovery Commitment

Love is a powerful adjunct in this process. An addict, a trauma survivor, and/or a mentally ill person has been operating at a love deficit due to the nature of their condition. These afflictions breed fear, confusion, and self-hatred. Love cannot get through without the opening provided by Sobriety, Safety, and/or Stability. So, as the second commitment, the power of Loving-kindness and specific care responses by professionals and family members takes hold. As one feels cared for and Loved, the opportunity for self-care arises, as well as the ability to be more Loving toward others. This is just what works. Exposure to this healing feeling is crucial. Get it now.

Love: The Number Two Recovery Value

This recovery process is not an easy road. It is as simple as 1,2,3,4,5.

Just not easy. The negative self-valuation that has accumulated over time has taken a toll. We come to a deep, dark hole of shame and despair. The way out includes large doses of Love. Kindness given in care settings such as treatment centers and clinics help get us through to the next phase. Self-kindness and self-compassion can develop over time and the good feelings of giving Loving-kindness to others is a delightful and uplifting experience. Love wins again.

Love Day:

So, a person gets Sober (addiction), Safe (trauma), and/or Stable (mental ills), and what happens next? Someone, usually a counselor in a treatment setting, steps up and says "I am with you in this and you can do it. We will walk together in this process and see it through". Encouragement is given. Clear, focused feedback is provided. A needed pat on the back, a hug, a smile, positive regard, all in the name of Love. We realized back in the 80's that we only wanted counselors on our staff who could honestly and genuinely serve in the most Loving way. We Love them until they can Love themselves. We celebrate their successes. We see them recover.

Love: The Second Recovery Commitment

Think of it this way: If you entered the recovery process and you had around you people who were emotionally manipulative, angry, crazy-making, and/or abusive, your chances of progressing would be diminished. It is imperative that you place yourself in an environment that is Loving and supportive to your well-being. Caring companions are your biggest advantage at this phase of recovery. Whether professional caregivers or family and friends, those who you are choosing to be with can make all the difference in your recovery.

Love: Second Level Recovery

When we talk about healing, we must talk about Love. Most everyone will acknowledge that Love has healing power. It is so much better than the absence of Love. In addiction, trauma, and mental illness, there exists perceptions by some others that are quite negative, blaming, and stigmatizing. These views must be overcome in order to be in any way helpful to those suffering these conditions. Not everyone can be helpful. Pick your caregivers and friends carefully. Be with the Lovers, not the hurters. Let Love be.

Love: The Second of the "Big Five Values" of Recovery

Ascending out of addiction, trauma, and/or mental disorder, we are left with a Love deficit. In order to move forward and upward on the recovery continuum we need to access as much Loving-kindness and genuine care as possible. Professional caregivers and naturally caring folks in our environment are available. It is important to avoid the crazy-makers and abusers. It is also very important to begin a program of self-care, doing all the best stuff to Love ourselves well. Eat right, get rest and good sleep, exercise, forgive yourself, be gentle with you, etc.

Love Day

Recovery is a process. The second phase of this process is by necessity Love. This is a major issue. Love is required due to the damage caused by addiction, trauma, and/or mental illness. That damage done is emotional, physical, social, and spiritual. The repair is brought about in large part when Love is prominent and prevalent. We respond favorably to Loving-Kindness from others. We slowly learn to Love ourselves. We eventually become Love givers.

Love: The Second Recovery Commitment

Once Sober, Safe, and/or Stable, it is time to commit to Love in order to move the recovery process forward. This means that we first open ourselves to the caring, support, encouragement, and positive regard coming from professional caregivers, family, and friends. These are the people who really care about our well-being and recovery. Then we start with a program of self-care. Then we reach out to help others. This Love thing is huge. You don't want to miss out.

Love

The Sober addict needs Love. The Safe trauma survivor needs Love. The Stabilized mentally ill needs Love. Love pushes one forward in the recovery process. The need for Love becomes so obvious once a person has entered this healing experience. To be cared for and soothed in a non-judgmental manner is such a blessing. Once a person knows they are valued, they can start valuing themselves and life itself. This value is enhanced over time with focus on Love. Just let Love flow. Allow Love to enter your realm. Love pays dividends.

Love: Recovery Value Two

"In every living thing there is a desire for love". -DH Lawrence

For those who have experienced the ravages of addiction, traumatic stress, and/or mental illness, this quote is especially true. There is an aspect of unlovability when active in these afflictions. Give Love to the one in need. Accept Love from all sources. Love heals.

Love Day

When an addict, a trauma survivor, or a mentally ill person enters a system of care, they will be cared for and Loved. Professional caregivers know that Love heals and encourages. Family and friends know that an effort is being made and they want to support that effort with Love. Early in the recovery process, Love is sustaining and motivating. Get it, give it, live it.

Chapter 3
Unity

Recovery value #3: Unity

This is the joining up phase of recovery. Involvement in a support group has proven to enhance positive outcomes. Research is clear in this regard. We don't need to traverse this path alone. There are many others further along in recovery who want to assist and share their wisdom. Hope is instilled when we access rooms with people who have recovered. We come to the realization that we are all connected. No longer alone, we can get this done. The commitment to group involvement is very important. It works.

Unity Day:

There is strength in numbers. We can do it, when I could not.

Finding a sense of belonging in a group of like-minded people counters the old feelings of isolation and separation so present in active addiction. It feels good to belong. We long to belong.

Connecting is what counts the most. It can be any support group or therapeutic network. AA and other 12-Step meetings are most prevalent and available, with meetings everywhere, everyday, morning, noon, and night. You get to hear some great stories, meet some wonderful people, and have some laughs. Oh, and you are provided your best chance for recovery.

Unity:
Have you ever experienced the power of a group hug? It is something not to be missed. Check it out sometime. Join up! There is a group of people, like you, waiting to share their hope and experience with you, who will not judge you or blame you. You will be welcomed and accepted. And helped. It is the human connection that counts.

Unity: The Third Commitment

The realization that I am not alone in my struggle and pain is huge. In addiction, trauma, and mental illness, the sense of separation and isolation is huge. So joining a support group is a way to overcome those devastating feelings of loneliness.

Some resist, insisting that going it alone will work, or is somehow more noble or fulfilling. The results are not so good without group connection. Committing to just showing up at meetings will work wonders. You will feel better. It is better to not let false pride to get in the way of success. Humility wins out every time. Just get with recovering folks and soak up the energy and solutions.

This boils down to you help me, I help you. All about giving and getting.

Unity: SlugStep #3

Walking into a support group for the first time can be intimidating for many. Often fears of judgment and rejection, based on past experiences, causes unease. This condition usually resolves itself soon enough. The realization occurs that these people are no different than me, that they have the best intentions, and they are after the same results. The self-consumed, scared new member is transformed into the smiling, helpful, experienced one in short order. All it takes is a commitment to show up and be present. The benefits are profound. However, you don't know that until you have the experience. This is something not to be missed.

Unity Day:

To be addicted, traumatized, or mentally ill, is to be isolated and alone in the struggle to cope and survive. Joining with others for mutual support and understanding is crucial to the process of recovery. Relief comes when one realizes that two or more engaging the struggle together brings better results. Shared experiences and hope serves to strengthen and motivate. Love gets spread around the room for all to derive benefit. Be part of the solution. It is self-help and mutual-help.

Unity: Level Three Recovery

At this level the commitment is around joining forces with fellow travelers on this road to full recovery. You find some in the rooms who have many years of experience traversing the path and who are more than willing to provide guidance, encouragement, and moral support. Then you find that there are some in the room who are newer than you, maybe they are scared and uncomfortable. At that point the opportunity to help another arises. You find out what you are made of and some of your purpose for being. A great sense of satisfaction can result.

Unity Day

Life before entering a recovery process was confusing and unpredictable much of the time. When engaged in a supportive network for recovery, that part changes. There is a real consistency and predictability in the mutual help meetings. They are always there. They have been there and will be there for you. You won't be rejected or hurt. Just supported and helped. You can count on it. A sign often posted at these meetings: "Hope is found here".

Unity Recovery Value # 3

The most important thing is to simply show up at the support group meetings. There is no pressure to talk or interact in any particular way. It is "bring the body and the mind will follow".
Especially early in the group attendance, just being there will offer what you need around instilling hope. Sometimes daily meetings are a necessity. With time, you will find a frequency that works best for you. Sometimes you will just know when you need to get to a meeting. Just don't quit before the miracle happens.

Unity Day:

Attending support groups provides the opportunity for guidance and the benefit of shared wisdom. A person with a specific problem, issue, or stuck point simply needs to put it out there to the group, and solutions will be offered. This sharing of experience enhances recovery for both the giver and receiver. This is the place where you give it away to keep it.

Unity: Commitment Three

Addiction, traumatic stress, and mental disorders bring much loneliness and separation from others. This isolated feeling is quite painful. In recovery, the opportunity to connect with a supportive network of like-minded people is one of the more powerful healing aspects of this model. Uniting with others who share in this effort is crucial. Giving and getting help moves one toward healing and happiness. Join up. Get in on the goodness.

Unity Day:

Belonging feels good. To walk into a room filled with people who understand and accept you feels great. The mutual support and kindness, the sharing of experiences and hope, the laughter and the tears, all make this an important part of the recovery process.

The wisdom and the faith will see you through the tougher times.

This commitment to group involvement solves the deep loneliness that is such a big part of addiction/trauma/mental disorders. Plus we can make some really good friends.

Unity: The Third Value/Commitment

There is much research that points to support group involvement as one of the indicators for positive recovery outcomes. When good studies show that some activity is effective, then we can feel assured that it is worth our time. Put in the time, and enjoy the benefits. Being part of a group made up of similar folks is worth it.

These people will not let you down. You will be lifted up

Unity Day:

Consider the meaning of friendship. What do you value most in a friend and what would you most offer others as a friend? Trust, openness, humor, fairness come to mind. What kind of person would you turn to in a time of need? What kind of friend do you want to be? Can you be counted on in a time of need?

Recovery support groups allow us to keep "wise company", and have good friends. This is solidarity and the power of community. With good friends, we have one of the greatest resources for happiness and freedom. We can count on these people.

Unity:

Addiction, traumatic stress, and mental disorders bring about a strong sense of separation and isolation. The recovery process from these conditions includes this reconnecting with others. The feeling of belonging to a group of like-minded people is in itself very healing. They are always there for me. No matter where I go, how long I've been away, what my condition is, they are there. It is a relief to have this kind of consistency and predictability in life. These people understand and accept, and they are not going to abandon or betray. Just how it is.

Unity: Level Three Recovery

When we join a support group, we are sharing an experience with millions of people across the globe. The 12 Step program phenomenon has been amazingly prolific and continues to function and grow for almost 80 years. Other groups exist to help recovering people to connect with fellow travelers on the path of healing and wholeness. The important thing is to commit. The benefits of shared wisdom and experience are huge. The hope and promise of a better tomorrow are real. Join up and rise up!

Unity: Recovery Value #3

In the group meetings that support recovery, you can bring up a particular problem or stuck point related to your process. What happens next is that others who have "been there, done that" will share what worked for them. Solutions abound. Sometimes just quietly being present, listening intently, you will receive wise counsel to help on the journey, without even asking. At times, there seems to be a spirit moving in the room, providing what is needed, right on time. Somewhat magical or even miraculous occurrences result. At conclusion, the meeting has provided just what is necessary to carry you further along the path to healing.

Unity Day:

So, what is it that we are united in? Well, we are first united by our condition, whether it is addiction, PTSD, or mental illness. This is a coming together due to a cause. Then there is being united by a purpose. The purpose for being in the room together is to access recovery. Hearing what others have gone through, and how they have overcome, is the shared experience that provides solutions. It is all about getting and giving help. When we help others, we help ourselves. Give and get. It is what works.

Unity: The Third Recovery Commitment

We all want to be seen, and heard, and feel a sense of belonging. In active addiction, traumatic stress, or mental disorders, we experience separation and isolation, and even invisibility. These painful states are overcome in this "joining up" phase of recovery. Once this commitment to group support is made and maintained, relief is profoundly experienced. I am seen. I am being heard. I belong. These people will be here for me. This problem is solved.

Unity Day:

We are united with a bond of shared Love. There are many and varied support groups available for help in overcoming addictions, traumatic stress, and mental disorders. The most important aspects are the mutuality, acceptance, understanding, and your commitment to active involvement. The SLUGS Model of Recovery provides another opportunity for mutual support. Discussing the "Big Five Values" in what I call "SLUGSessions" can keep us focused on our priorities and enhance our healing journey.

Unity: The third of the "Big Five" for Recovery

Entering a room with support group members present brings a sense of belonging and connectedness based on our similarities and common goal. We understand and accept one another. The fact is that the connection goes beyond this room, this town, this state, this country.
This recovery thing is worldwide. There are literally millions of people in this boat. We are united in the effort to recover. There is a "New Recovery Movement" taking place today worldwide. Welcome to the club. It is truly a great thing.

Unity Day:

Finding a connection with other people who have similar challenges is what the third phase of the recovery process is about. This process is a lot about giving and getting help. The founders of AA, the grandfather of support groups, discovered that the best way to help their self was to reach out and help others. "You have to give it away to keep it". We are also defined and shaped by the company we keep. Keep good company and experience the joy and enthusiasm of this glorious sharing of love.

Unity: Recovery commitment #3

Research clearly indicates that support group involvement leads to better outcomes. Those who commit and participate recover at a much higher rate than those who attempt recovery on their own. In a very practical sense, the group members who have had struggles with certain issues, and successfully overcome them, can serve as guides for others. "Here is what I did, and this worked for me" can be very helpful in a time of need. My efforts and accomplishments can and do benefit others. It is all about sharing these experiences. It is about sharing strength gained. It is about shared hope and love.

Unity Day:

We join a support group in order to get that support and to feel that sense of belonging that is absent when addicted, traumatized, or mentally unstable. The Unity feeling can and does, if allowed, extend beyond the group or individuals to whom we are currently committed. We are able to feel a real connection to all recovering people in the world. We can sense being part of all humanity and united with all living beings. This Unity thing has many layers and can be as broad and wide as one desires. We are United. The Universe is not apart from anyone. That is why it is called Universe. Embrace and engage.

Unity: The Third Recovery Commitment

There is strength in numbers. I can accomplish with the help of others what I could not accomplish alone. There is no shame in asking for and accepting help. The important thing is around reaching the goal. Research supports support group involvement. Why resist?

It is not more noble to go it alone. To enter a mutual help group experience is to take a step toward health and wholeness. You also get the great benefit from being a real assist to others. Feels good.

Unity: Level Three Recovery

Getting to the third level of recovery means that a period of Sobriety, Safety, and/or Stability has been achieved. The addict, trauma victim, or mentally disturbed has some benefit of loving kindness and caring that has brought some amount of healing. Joining a support group is an opportunity to further the process. The shared group wisdom and additional grounding in

recovery principles helps solidify the progress. The feeling of belonging and common experience allows for an overcoming of the sense of isolation that is so prevalent in these states of disorder.
We can embrace the sense of oneness and relax into a healing community that truly understands and accepts.

Unity Day

No question about it. This recovery thing is difficult, as in really hard to accomplish, evidenced by the numbers of people who do not make it. The fact is, and this is really important, doing recovery together makes it easier. Think about it this way: if you were trying to push a heavy object up a hill, and it was more than you alone could accomplish, would you accept the help of a fellow traveler? If you wanted to succeed in meeting the goal, you would. We together can accomplish what I alone could not. The point is to get to where we want to be. Again, and the research supports this, doing recovery together makes it easier. We have this. We can do it.

Unity: The Third Recovery Commitment

This phase of recovery is like an extension of Love, in that it is now being given freely in a group setting. The support groups that function to provide guidance and assistance in the recovery process are filled with people who care. They care to get well. And they care for the other group members, knowing that their healing is somewhat dependent on helping others. It just works that way. So, making this commitment to joining up is crucial and provides a sense of belonging that was not available previously. The connectivity with others who are aspiring to health and wholeness brings fulfillment.

Unity Day:

When we join others in this support group experience, we realize that we are not alone. The degree of loneliness in addiction, trauma, and mental illness is extreme. This overcoming of separation is profoundly important. An opportunity is born. We can see that we are all more alike than different. I can help you while you help me. You understand what I am going through. I accept you as you are, and you do the same for me. This recovery thing is possible, and much more likely, if we are together working on it. Join up. Rise up.

Unity: The Third Recovery Value

Separation, isolation, secrecy, rejection, and judgment are all hallmarks of addiction, traumatic stress, and mental illness. This is a painful reality. The overcoming phase of all this lonely existence is around the joining with others who are focused on recovery and the journey to wellness and wholeness. There are wonderful, open support groups available in practically every community designed to provide the necessary ingredients for success in this endeavor. When you first walk into one of these rooms, you will feel the love and acceptance. They are there awaiting your arrival. Come on in.

Unity Day:

A common practice in support groups is the exchange of phone numbers. The primary purpose is around making a call when in need of immediate support outside of the actual meeting time. This can be a life-saving measure. Who to call, my drug dealer or my recovery mentor? The choice is ours to make based on our own determination and commitment to the recovery process. We have gotten Sober, Safe, and/or Stable. We have experienced Love and mutual support. Do we choose to move forward toward Growth and lasting peace, or do we regress? Choose wisely when making that call. Save a life.

Unity: Level Three Recovery

Acceptance, concern, encouragement, forgiveness, belonging, hope, direction, support, all given freely in the rooms of the groups for recovery. Entering this world of positivity after years of extreme negative experience is a true lifeline. Those who have long term recovery are ready and willing to help, sharing what has worked for them in moving toward wholeness and real health. Peace prevails in this realm and is spread around. This is a profound and very important part of the overall solution. Be certain to join up. Recovery takes place when we find the proper folks to hang with. Hang tough.

Unity: The Third of the "Big Five Values" of Recovery

Joining up, uniting with others in the recovery process, is a very important step. We get help and we give help. We support and are supported. We learn and we teach. We belong. We are no longer isolated and alone. We have clarity of purpose. We get on the freedom train with these fellow travelers. Welcome to the club.

Unity Day

Research shows that people with regular attendance at support group meetings experience recovery at a significantly higher rate. That is the most important thing to know about the third commitment.

It is also important to know that much wisdom, a "folk wisdom", is found in these rooms of support. Those in long-term recovery have much of that depth of experience to share with those just joining. It is an aspect of this process that must not be missed. Unity works.

Unity

Research shows that people with regular attendance at support group meetings experience recovery at a significantly higher rate. That is the most important thing to know about the third commitment.

It is also important to know that much wisdom, a "folk wisdom", is found in these rooms of support. Those in long-term recovery have much of that depth of experience to share with those just joining. It is an aspect of this process that must not be missed. Unity works.

Unity: The Third Recovery Commitment

Shame causes us to feel isolated and abandoned, as if we don't belong. The prevailing support groups that are widely available are most likely a safe place to share and experience connection. This promotes healing. We are helped and we help others, realizing that all who are present are in need. We are all vulnerable. We all have shame. We all are deserving of assistance and care. Joining forces with others who are like us, who accept and understand us, is essential. This commitment contributes to full recovery.

Unity: The Number Three Recovery Value

Gathering together in a room with like-minded travelers on the path to recovery brings an empowering feeling. I can share my experience without fear of judgment or condemnation. I can offer support and understanding to others. I can learn how to cope with specific challenges. I can overcome my shyness and reluctance. This place is conducive to change. These people care and they want to gain wellness. They want only the highest good for me. Where I need and want to be.

Unity Day:

Thank Goodness for the 12 Step programs and other support groups available to aid in the recovery process. It is hard to imagine a world without them. Any addict, trauma survivor, or mentally ill person would simply be without one of the greatest resources for healing. The idea of being singularly left on our own to figure out the way to wellness is unfathomable at this point. The true spiritual community, with its loving presence and consistency, provides just what is needed to bring us to the next phase of personal development. The result is more self-confidence and the ability and willingness to help others. This is a method to overcome these serious afflictions.

Unity: The Third Recovery Commitment

Joining forces with others leads to success in recovery. We find that there is power in numbers. The more we connect with fellow recovering addicts, trauma survivors, or recovering mentally ill, the more likely positive outcomes will result. So, going to support group meetings, getting contact information from fellow attendees, actually contacting people when necessary, and being there for them, all contributes to recovery. We give and get support. The group succeeds together and love is spread around the room. Soak it up.

Unity: Third Level Recovery

When we join a support group, we are committing to giving and getting acceptance and understanding that is really not available anywhere else. These are like-minded folks with similar life experiences and similar goals. We pull together to accomplish these goals. We win by being totally in this thing together. The possibility of full recovery from addiction, traumatic stress, and/or mental ills is greatly enhanced by attending regular meetings. This just works.

Unity: The Third of the "Big Five Values" of Recovery

The isolation and self-centeredness that is present with active addiction, traumatic stress, and mental illness tends to linger on and becomes an impediment to recovery. The solo route is preferred due to our fear of others, the fear of intimacy. Overcoming this resistance is crucial to long-term recovery. Becoming a member of a support group will build trust in the process and enhance the opportunity for full recovery. Join up, rise up, and experience the power of "We."

Unity Day

Joining forces with others active in the recovery process is an empowering experience. "I" becomes "we". We are in this thing together and we can definitely overcome addiction, traumatic stress, and/or mental illness. It is evident that long term recovery is possible and even likely due to the number of people who have gone before us. They are in the rooms. Their legacy and solutions live on. The basic folk wisdom is present and applicable today and every day.

Unity: The Third Recovery Commitment

impact on a newer member. When that long timer says "I was really sick. I came in here frightened and without hope for a better life. This program saved me. Life is wonderful. I am healthy and happy now." The person just getting started in recovery can latch on to these words and launch into a healing adventure. This is some of what works in this process.

Unity

The recovering addict needs Unity with fellow recovering addicts. The trauma survivor needs Unity with fellow recovering trauma survivors. The recovering mentally ill needs Unity with fellow recovering mentally ill. This support is crucial to the process of ongoing recovery and the achievement of long-term recovery. The fellow travelers understand, accept, and guide you. You do the same for them. It is give and get. Get in order to give. Give to get.

Unity: Recovery Value Three

Some people resist joining a support group. This attempt to "go it alone" is foolhardy and unlikely to yield benefit. The likely motivation in this avoidance of group support is around pride and ego saying solo is somehow preferred. The do-it-yourself path can lead to relapse. Why not rely on the success of others to assist. The important thing is to access long-term recovery. Research tells us that involvement in mutual-help groups improves recovery outcomes. Hang with winners and learn to win. It is that simple.

Unity Day

Once a person is Sober, Safe, and/or Stable, and then they start experiencing
Love, this process of recovery is moved forward through joining a support
group of others with similar afflictions. The importance of this action cannot
be overstated. With the sense of isolation and separation that comes with
addiction, traumatic stress, and mental illness, the need to feel togetherness
and belonging is paramount. So, looking around the room, hearing others
stories, one comes to know "these are my people". We are in this together.

Chapter 4
Growth

Recovery value #4: Growth

This phase involves a commitment to self-improvement activities. Examples of growth enhancing practices are: therapy for family of origin issues (most addicts have had adverse childhood experiences like an addicted parent, abuse, abandonment, betrayal, etc.), working the 12 Steps, body work (exercise/nutrition), reading self-help material, etc. Life becomes a self-improvement project. Affirmation: "Every day, in every way, I am getting better and better".

Growth Day:

Getting better, weller than well, being all that you can be, doing our best, room for improvement, expansion, accomplishing goals, ascending to a higher realm, being fit, being happy; all of this and more speaks to personal growth as an essential element in the recovery process.

Do I need to be more patient, kind, or calm? It can and will be done. A commitment to self-improvement pays dividends.

Just get started. You don't yet know how good it can get.

Growth:

This is an adventurous part of the healing journey. There is new learning, self-discovery, and development of coping skills. Therapy for family of origin (foo) issues pays off. We get to understand from where a lot of these challenges originate. So many of us had big hurt as children. We need to fully explore and resolve this stuff. Accessing resources for positive change becomes routine .We find ourselves seeking out growth enhancing experiences. Self-improvement activities, and the tangible results, becomes kind of addictive. Enjoy the ride. A new day has arrived. A new you is emerging.

Growth: The Fourth Commitment

This is the work phase of recovery and the payoff is significant.

You get a chance to experience the joy of resolving long standing emotional issues and just feeling better about life and yourself.

So, if you need to clean up your diet, get more exercise, or learn to relax, it is time to begin. Real change comes when we follow through day to day. Make these efforts part of your daily routine.

Working the 12 Steps brings growth, for certain. Practicing new coping skills, developing talents, and following your dreams are all ways of growing. Life is a self improvement project.

Growth: SlugStep #4

A lot of this growth stuff occurs naturally once one gets sober, gets love, and gets mutual help in the support group. You are better off due to the first three recovery values/commitments.

There is also now more motivation to improve you, and there are plenty of opportunities. Reading self-help material, practicing relaxation techniques, getting therapy, self-examination, and helping others are all things that start to happen effortlessly.

It is fun to improve. Meet the challenge of becoming a better you.

Growth Day:

When one is stuck in an addiction, traumatic stress, or emotional/mental distress, there is no room for growth. It is a static, stuck place that leads to deterioration or general decline.

Recovery boosts us up toward a more complete and rewarding life experience. We are challenged to strengthen and expand. As we experience growth, we want to have more of it. It becomes a self-fulfilling motivational force. Everything happening in our lives can be used as a means for growth. So, get going and get growing.

Growth: Level Four Recovery

Commitment to self-improvement pays off with constancy and repetition. If we perform a particular activity over time, over and over, we certainly are going to get better at it. In this program, to have a daily routine around these growth activities, staying true to that routine, we will notice significant progress. So, self-examination, exercise, working the 12 Steps, stretching, deep breathing, seeing a therapist, taking a class, doing art, keeping a journal, all are examples of this level. There are many more. The most important part is following through on the commitment to practice and repetition.

Growth Day

One major purpose of this phase of recovery is to resolve family of origin (foo) issues. Adverse childhood experiences leave a lasting impact on who we are and how we function/cope. These are best explored in therapy and through the development of new skills for self-regulation of problem moods and/or behaviors. Foo issues linger and affect our relationships in negative ways. Recovery is enhanced when we accept the truth about our early life experience and make changes accordingly. Much will be revealed. It is an ongoing process.

Growth: Recovery Value # 4

It is often said "there is always room for improvement". That is what Level Four Recovery is about. Looking at ourselves objectively, considering others feedback, we ask where we need to improve ourselves. Are negative emotional states or distorted thoughts causing difficulties? Do relationships need work? Am I as fit and healthy as possible? We can work on ourselves in so many different ways. Self-improvement or personal growth simply requires a commitment to practice new behavior until the change takes hold. It is worth the effort. Keep going and keep growing.

Growth Day:

This is the "working on oneself" phase of recovery. The desire for self-improvement appears universal. We get better at living a quality life by practicing high quality behaviors. How can I be a better friend? How can I become calm and focused? What changes do I need to make in order to accomplish my goals? Where do I need to focus my efforts for self growth?

Answering questions like these help give direction. This is about striving for progress, not perfection. Better is as better does.

Growth: Commitment Four

Making certain activities part of our daily routine is a route to personal growth. One such activity is keeping a journal of thoughts, feelings, events, and goals. This will serve to guide us and allow for recording the growth path that we are on. Reflecting back on where we were and how far we have come is a motivational force. Just commit to this activity and do it every day. The benefit is more clarity and direction. It is often fun. Enjoy. The more you know, the more you grow. Self-knowledge helps.

Growth Day:

In what ways do we grow in recovery? We grow in our capacity to love. We grow in our understanding of ourselves. We grow in our ability to accept change in life. We grow in knowledge and wisdom. We grow in peace. We grow in so many ways by working a program that includes self-examination, self-honesty, a willingness to put forth the effort, reading self-help material, getting therapy for family-of-origin issues, working the 12 Steps, exercising, refining diet, breathing deeply, and staying focused on our needs for self-improvement. Recovery is adventuresome.

Growth: The Fourth Value/Commitment

Personal growth starts with taking a good, honest look at ourselves. Part of the process includes being open to the feedback of others. If we consistently hear from others that some aspect of ourselves is offensive or troublesome, it is time to consider changing it up. If self-doubt, jealousy, fear, anger, or other negative emotional states continue to impact our relationships, it is time for effort around improving ourselves. Getting better every day is a noble goal. And it is achievable.

Growth Day:

In this phase of recovery, we have embraced the idea that life is a self-improvement project. We are here, in this life, making mistakes and missteps, wanting to do better. For full recovery from addiction, trauma, or mental disorders, we need to be working on ourselves from here on out. Never stop growing. It is essential to this process and to an enjoyable life experience. So, each day is a new beginning. We can do this thing. Recovery is an inside job. Focus on what can be worked on today. Do it now.

Growth:

When we get to this level of recovery, we begin to bring forth more effort. Some growth is happening just through being at this point in recovery. Further personal growth requires focusing on areas of self that can use improvement. We discover that remaining the same is not workable. My relationships may need special attention. My method of communicating my needs and desires can be better. Being more honest and forthcoming, being more present, connecting in a deeper way, are all important. Enjoy the journey of personal growth. Getting better every day.

Growth: Level Four Recovery

When we grow in recovery, we are fulfilling a purpose and promise of life. We are here to grow. One profound method for personal growth is psychotherapy. Most of us have family of origin (FOO) issues that can be overpowering. Depression and anxiety can result, and this can be deadly. These things can be worked out with professional help. Individual and group therapy are available. Reading self-help books is also recommended. This level involves risk and takes courage. Everything else has prepared you to accept this challenge. At Level Four you are ready to do this.

Growth: Recovery Value #4

As the recovery process moves along, we sometimes find ourselves struggling with emotional issues that seemingly arise from nowhere. It is like we have recycled back to the old pre-recovery state with fear, self-doubt, anger, confusion, or depression. This is a time to increase our effort around getting to the source of these troubling emotions. Therapy, honest self-examination, talking it out, reading, working the program, all will lead to a return to active recovery. Pushing through the tough time is growth enhancing. We come out the other side stronger.

Growth Day:

We grow by committing to and engaging in a variety of self-improvement activities. Growth is also realized just by showing up for our life responsibilities and pushing through the tough stuff, the challenges of every day existence and meeting the new tests that life naturally brings. This meeting of life on life's terms, and achieving our goals, is cause for celebration. We are making our life with a quality and purpose that did not manifest previously. This is proof that recovery is worth the effort. Go on and grow on.

Growth: The Fourth Recovery Commitment

How do we measure Growth in recovery? There are numerous ways to look at how life is improving through this process. We can mark the amount of time Sober, Safe, or Stable. Fewer, or less frequent, negative emotional events or distorted thoughts are good indicators of progress. We just feel better. We are more energized. Relationship functioning improves. No jail or emergency room visits. Spring is in your step. More smiling happens. Self-confidence enhanced.

You just know that this thing called recovery is working for you.

Growth Day:

When we go through tough times, we grow. When we face loss and sorrow, we experience growth. Staying Sober, Safe (for trauma), and/or Stable (mental ills) brings about growth. We are growing when we Love ourselves and others. We grow by working the 12 Steps. Psychotherapy promotes growth. Committing to a daily exercise routine is growth enhancing. Nutrition awareness and healthy lifestyles grow us. Letting go of resentment and fear allows us to grow. Life is a self-improvement project. Grow n glow.

Growth: The Fourth of the "Big Five" for Recovery

In recovery, when we experience Growth, it is proof that this effort is bringing lasting benefit. We grow in wellness. We grow in confidence. We grow in integrity. We grow in loving-kindness. We grow in clarity and focus. We grow in acceptance. We grow in calmness. We grow in personal empowerment. We grow in so many ways. Often others see it first and point out how we have changed for the better. This is cause for celebration. How long was it all going the other way? It is great to be on a Growth path.

Growth Day:

This phase of the recovery process is the working on oneself part. It does require work and effort. When engaging in psychotherapy, for example, reaching down into the depths of our past experiences and grappling with those realities and traumas is essential. Nothing easy about it. Sometimes painful stuff arises. Then we work through and come out the other side all the better and stronger. We work on ourselves emotionally, physically, mentally, and spiritually. Work pays dividends. Empowerment results. We are better prepared for life challenges. Work it.

Growth: Recovery Commitment #4

This is a most active phase of the recovery process. Our commitment is to engage in activities that promote self-improvement. Some examples are psychotherapy, exercise, reading self-help material, working the 12 Steps, nutritional refinement, and self-examination. We can and do get better over time with these measures and more. Experiment and find ways to enhance your life experience. What was once a life of decline transforms into a life of Growth. We become better and better through recovery. Celebrate the new and emerging person that you have become, growing healthier, calmer, stronger, more clear and focused each and every day.

Growth Day:

When it comes to getting better, patience is key. We must be patient with ourselves. Sometimes this is two steps forward, one step back.

It is important to allow for the natural pace of these changes. It is not something that can be forced. Life brings challenges and problems to solve, which brings growth.

A couple of relevant quotes for you:

"Adopt the pace of nature, her secret is patience". Ralph W. Emerson

"Be patient and tough; someday this pain will be useful to you". Ovid

Growth: The Fourth Recovery Commitment

Self-improvement and an overall enhanced quality of life are by-products of this process of recovery. We are better able to handle the challenges that life brings, and we notice distinct improvement in our relationships. People notice when we are getting better. They respond to us in a more positive manner. They say "you have changed", "you seem happier, calmer, more attentive". We do the required self-examination and realize that we have less of the negative traits and feelings that weighed us down before. Life has become lighter, freer, more manageable, more peaceful. Growth is good. And these changes, this improvement, is never ending.

Growth: Level Four Recovery

Growth comes naturally to one who has become Sober (Safe for trauma, Stable for mental ills), Loved/Loving, and United. All is just better. Then we choose to focus on enhancing our quality of life by working on ourselves, knowing that life is indeed a self-improvement project. We become more honest. We get into better shape, physically and mentally. We improve our relationships and communication. We address any second addiction or lingering issues around trauma or mental disorder. We confront family of origin issues with professional help. We plan for a glorious future and happiness.

Growth Day

There is truth to the saying that "if we are not growing, we are regressing". This recovery value is essential to prevent relapse and a return to the suffering of active addiction, traumatic stress, and/or mental instability. Growth starts with honest self-examination. The 12 Step programs speak of taking a personal inventory. Where in me is the need for self-improvement? So, getting therapy for our family of origin issues, working the 12 Steps, practicing relaxation techniques, reading self-help articles and books, and asking others for feedback are all helpful, growth oriented practices. Personal growth can be an adventurous experience. We discover who we are and what we are capable of becoming. Life expands and is enriched. Have at it.

Growth: The Fourth Recovery Commitment

The commitment to Growth comes along after we have engaged in getting Sober, Safe, and/or Stable, gotten Love, and United with others. We are already Growing and ready to Grow more. We set goals. We become stronger in many ways. Issues get resolved. Fear gets faced and overcome. Insecurity leaves us. Confidence returns. The self we were meant to become is emerging. Happiness encroaches on our life experience. We find relaxation. We find motivation. All is better. Life starts to make sense. We can see the Light. We feel free and we express a passion for life. Live it fully!

Growth Day:

This phase of the recovery process involves taking action around improving aspects of oneself. We all have room for improvement. We have seen that certain behaviors or attitudes have been harmful, or at least not conducive to self-respect or good feelings. So we change it up. We take responsibility, doing things that make us feel good about ourselves, and not doing things that make us feel bad about ourselves. These things have to do with exercise, diet, psychotherapy, rest and relaxation, nurturing, learning, laughing, loving, and more. Practice and repetition works. Go grow now.

Growth: The Fourth Recovery Value

A person in long-term recovery is a completely different person than they were previously. Inside and out, top to bottom, different, improved in every way. Just ask them to tell you about it. Just ask those closest to them. The changes are dramatic and profound. Growth happens in recovery, naturally, and with some effort. At a recent support group meeting, someone had a shirt on with the saying "Grow or die". Life may very well depend on Growth for those afflicted with these conditions. "Grow and really live".

Growth Day:

The commitment to Growth can also be life-saving. The fact is that addiction, traumatic stress, and mental illness all have shame as a core issue to be resolved. Toxic shame, chronic shame, triggered shame, spiraling shame, binding, hurtful, scary shame can take us down. Deep depression can result, leading to self-destruction. So, committing to learning about shame, confronting and conquering shame through long-term psychotherapy and self-help, discovering your true self and loving who you are, gives the opportunity to grow past this huge issue. Make the effort to successfully address shame. We all deserve relief from this barrier to happiness. Be compassionate with yourself. Grow to fully heal and enjoy life.

Growth: Level Four Recovery

Self improvement often involves honest self-examination, whereas in active addiction there was often honest self-deception (denial). One way to enhance the process is by journaling. When we write about our experiences, thoughts, and feelings, we can see a pattern emerge and we can more readily mark progress made. Writing forces us to locate our clarity. Clarity starts when we have been Sober, Safe, and/or Stable earlier in recovery. We continue to get a clear and better view of ourselves and circumstances as we Grow.

Growth: The Fourth of the "Big Five Values" of Recovery

We find out that self-improvement is within our own power. We can indeed get better, in any and every way, with the application of our own effort. There is so much in life outside of our control. We each get to decide, and act on, these aspects of life around therapy, exercise, nutrition, patience, kindness, reading, reflecting, resting, relaxing, and relating. We can improve ourselves in so many ways. Life is indeed a self-improvement project. Progress, not perfection.

Growth Day

The entire recovery experience is about positive change. The sickness changes to wellness. The loneliness changes to connection. The unable part changes to empowerment. The guilt and shame changes to self-acceptance. These changes come with time and effort. Each stage of the recovery process brings with it specific change points. It is through embracing this process that we improve our lives and functioning. So many miraculous changes occur in recovery. You will truly be amazed. Go for it. Grow for it. Grow you.

Growth: The Fourth Recovery Commitment

Growth becomes a lifelong commitment in the recovery process. We know that we must be involved in self-improvement activities or we regress. So, psychotherapy for family of origin issues and the healing of shame, reading and applying self-help materials, working the 12 Steps, exercising and nutrition refinement, self-examination and attitudinal assessment and adjustment, all are helpful. Getting better every day is what it is about. Grow on.

Growth: The Number Four Recovery Value

At this phase of the recovery process we can review how we have Grown so far. The suffering of active addiction, traumatic stress, and/or mental disorders has diminished. We feel a sense of freedom that eluded us previously. The burden is lighter. We have more hope and confidence. Plans for the future are being made and realized and relationships have stabilized. Positive change is obvious in our moods and behaviors. We know that the promise is for more good to come. Enjoy working on your self. The benefits are great.

Growth Day:

We learn and grow from our mistakes. No failure is final, as long as we are breathing. The purpose of life is to love and learn and find peace. This recovery process is all about fulfilling that purpose. These principles set in motion a process that allows for mistakes, that allows for learning, that allows for personal development, that brings us ultimately to a peaceful existence. So, when we get Sober, and we rediscover Love, and we Unite with others in recovery, we are definitely on a Growth path. This is cause for celebration.

Growth: The Fourth Recovery Commitment

This level of recovery challenges us to become better. We want to be better at being who we are, how we function in the world, how we perform in our relationships and various life roles. There is an opportunity to improve every aspect of our lives. By being engaged in the process of recovery, we are doing self-examination daily. We have an awareness of where we need work on ourselves. Doing this work brings great benefit. We progress. We recover. We become the self we were meant to be. Our true self emerges. Better and best.

Growth: Fourth Level Recovery

"Everyday, in everyway, I am getting better and better". This becomes the reality of our new life experience. We can learn from our mistakes and know that all of life offers improvement opportunities. The fact that we are still here, doing the life we have been given, is proof that progress can and will be made. Long term recovery from addiction, traumatic stress, and/or mental ills provides continuous Growth. This is a wonderful thing.

Growth: The Fourth of the "Big Five Values" of Recovery

An increase in self-confidence is a sign of Growth. Self-consciousness, self-doubt, and fear seem to fade away with the ongoing recovery process. So we become more willing to try new things, accept new challenges, and do further work on ourselves. The pain and negativity related to past experiences has diminishing power over time. We can relax into the knowing that life is on an improvement track and all is on time as it relates to our Growth.

Growth Day

We are talking about changing aspects of our behavior and committing to action that brings about positive change. As we do honest self-reflection, we see where we need to focus our work. Family of origin issues usually get our attention and these require psychotherapy over a long term. We may need to work on our physical selves with a program of exercise and nutrition change. We may need to practice relaxation techniques or learn new communication skills. It is all worth the time and effort. Get busy.

Growth: The Fourth Recovery Commitment

This whole idea around self-improvement gains in importance as we move through the recovery process. We realize that getting Sober (Safe for trauma, Stable for mental ills), getting Love, and getting United has brought us to a whole new place in life in terms of better. We find that working the 12 Steps, getting psychotherapy, exercising, breathing deeply and stretching, practicing patience, and learning new coping skills, all lead to dramatic personal development. We still and always have room to improve. Life is like that. It is all good.

Growth

The recovering addict needs to Grow. The recovering trauma survivor needs to Grow. The recovering mentally ill needs to Grow. Personal Growth is a factor in ongoing and full recovery. We need to know that we are getting better. This effort around self-improvement is not wasted. We become better communicators. We become more honest and authentic. We become better listeners. We become better parents, friends, and lovers. We live life to the fullest and do not regret the past. We embrace change and go with the flow and Grow. Better and better, a new way, a new day.

Growth: Recovery Value Four

Getting better requires work. We are a work in progress. The effort put forth in improving ourselves physically, mentally, emotionally, socially, and spiritually enhances our quality of life. It also contributes to long-term recovery from addiction, traumatic stress, and mental disorders. Self-improvement makes us feel better about ourselves. That is a pretty important outcome. Don't settle for less.

Growth Day

One of the areas of obvious Growth in recovery is humility. We come to a realization that we are indeed human, we make mistakes, we learn from those mistakes, and that our own selfish needs or desires do not override the needs of others. We find more compassion in our hearts. We discover a calm patience that never seemed available previously. Life takes on a different look and feel around its unfolding and we are able to overcome the burden of ego dominance.

Chapter 5
Spirituality

Recovery value #5: Spirituality

Prayer and meditation. Reading inspiring material. Letting go of control. Living in the here and now. An attitude of gratitude. Surrender to a higher power. Deep breathing. Mindfulness.

These practices indicate a commitment to spirituality and total recovery. Research is clear on the benefits. We all share in the goal of peace-of-mind. May you find it now. Quote: "I am not chairman of the outcomes committee".

Spirituality Day:

Call it God, call it the Universe, call it Authentic Self, call it Allah, call it Buddha Nature, or call it Whatever. Whatever "It" is, pray to It, allow It to provide guidance and peace. Walk in the light of the Spirit and embrace Its soothing presence. Let go. Let it be.

Prayer: "Thank You for all these blessings. Thanks for perfect health and wellbeing, thanks for my divinely appointed job, thanks for inner peace and security, thanks for right companionship and love, thanks for abundant supply and prosperity".

Spirituality:

Today is a gift. Life itself is a gift. Grateful to be alive and have a chance to thrive. Breathe deeply. Encouraging and inspiring others is a spiritual act. Being fully present is spiritual. Total acceptance is spiritual. Letting go is spiritual action. All is unfolding as it should. Inner peace is yours for keeps. May you find it now. "Aspire to Inspire before you Expire!", Eugene Bell, Jr.

Spirituality: The Fifth Commitment

This phase of recovery involves a willingness to explore the mysteries of life, to delve into the depths of meaning. Seek answers to questions like:

What does it mean to be in the flow of life?
Who really has control here? Who is driving this bus?
What would happen if I truly let go?

What am I here to accomplish? What is my divinely appointed job?
So, embrace the process, release the outcome. Engage.
Practice living in the now. Surrender to what is.
Pray, meditate, give thanks. Find your true Self. Become whole.

Spirituality: SlugStep #5

Some of the things people say:
"It's a God deal", "It is all One", "All is perfect and on time".
Other related thoughts:
Living life with purpose. Finding peace. Divine inspiration.

A prayer:
I am at one with the power that manifests my desires.

Spirituality Day:

Prayer and meditation are the foundations of a spiritual practice. There are
many varieties of these practices. A simple prayer of thanks does wonders for
our attitude. A simple few minutes of quiet contemplation does wonders for
our mood. The goal is inner peace. Practice, practice, practice. Be here, now.

Trust the power of the Source of all good working in your life.

Turn it over. Let go of worry. Let go of control. Let go of the illusion of
control. Clothe yourself in a robe of light representing the power of universal
truth and goodness.

Spirituality: Level Five Recovery

In Level Five we come to the realization that much of what has transpired was
not of our doing. That forces beyond us brought us forward to where we are
today. So many circumstances and events are out of our realm of control. We
are truly blessed to have survived and now have achieved some amount of
peace and contentment. People have come and gone in our life for our
benefit. We give thanks to the Source. We pray for guidance. We walk in the
light of the Spirit.

Spirituality Day

Considering life from a spiritual perspective, some mystery persists. We can wonder how we arrived at this place, with these people, with this hope, having had all of these difficulties and trials. How is it that recovery is a reality and some semblance of peace is present. Addiction, trauma, and/or mental illness once was prevalent, with all of the corresponding confusion and pain. What happened?

Answer: Grace intervened.

Spirituality: Recovery Value # 5

Nurture your spirit in these ways and more:

Focus attention on your breathing. Be fully present. Experience nature. Express gratitude. Spend quality time with a child. Pray.
Don't hang out with people who try to kill your spirit. There are those of low spiritual essence. who want to bring you down. Spend time with the joyous and free spirits who want only your highest good. Know that you are on the right path.

Spirituality Day:

As we learn and practice the art of letting go, we move into the realm of accepting all that is, as it is. Serenity is often challenged by changing circumstances and the upheavals of life. Releasing the illusion of control is the solution. The idea of control over another person, and their choices, is problematic and leads to suffering. Embrace change, accept all, and keep the faith. A plan is in place to take each of us to a higher level when we let go.

Spirituality: Commitment Five

What does it mean to have a relationship to a Higher Power?
It means "I am not chairman of the outcomes committee."
It means letting go and allowing the good to manifest naturally in life, allowing life to flow without my futile efforts to control.
Relax into the goodness of divine order, accepting all.
Quotes: "Thy will, not mine, be done." "There, but for the Grace of God, go I." If we pray, meditate, and read inspiring material, we find our way home to true peace. Let it be.

Spirituality Day:

This is about a yearning for awakening. It is natural to live a life of higher consciousness. We are meant to soar! Through honesty, trust, gratitude, and acceptance, we get to the place we want to be. It is a gradual process of making progress. We come to a sense of wholeness. We become a new self. We are more complete. We are free to be. We live in peace in the here and now.

Spirituality: The Fifth Value/Commitment

What is it that we are committing to in this phase of recovery? We are first committing to practice. We practice a new way of responding to the world and all of the various happenings. We learn, with practice, to accept that pleasure and pain, gain and loss, praise and blame constantly arise and pass away, beyond our control. Acceptance of what is, taking things as they come, and allowing others to be, is a way to peace. Peace of mind is the goal we all share.

Practicing spiritual principles will take you home.

Spirituality Day:

Arriving at this stage of the recovery process means that Sobriety (or Safety/Stability), Love, Unity, and Growth have had the profound influence of bringing us to a place of understanding. We know that Grace and Truth prevail. A Power is functioning to guide life and our individual choices henceforth. Through prayer, meditation, inspirational reading, and an attitude of gratitude, we achieve a calmness never experienced before. We accept that life has a natural and beneficial flow to it. All is well and in the right direction. Patience and humility rules the day.

Spirituality:

At Level Five of this recovery model is where we find true peace and wholeness of being. The process involves maturing spiritually and awakening spiritually. We fully realize all of the gifts that have been and are being provided. Gratitude takes hold. Prayers of thanks, coupled with meditative sessions, bring broad benefit. At this level of recovery, the presence of a Higher Power operating in our life for our ultimate good is indisputable. What a great day!

Spirituality: Level Five Recovery

Living in the light of the spirit means accepting life as it is unfolding, going along with the flow of life, if you will. This requires faith. Accept everything. We have no control over events or other people anyway. At this level of recovery, there is an ease, a calmness which prevails more and more. Prayer and meditation, being with nature, living in the now, gratitude, letting go, all help us to reach a place of sustaining peace. Keep the faith, and it will keep you. Guidance is available for the asking.

Spirituality: Recovery Value #5

This healing journey takes us from a place of being sick, lonely, unable, guilt, and shame (lower s.l.u.g.s.), to a place of Sobriety, Love, Unity, Growth, and Spirituality (Higher S.L.U.G.S.). This is truly nothing less than a whole-person transformation. Some call it a miracle. It is cause for celebration. The significance of this great event cannot be minimized. Blessings abound, all around. Being wholly grateful is most appropriate. Fulfilled and thrilled.

Spirituality Day:

This level of recovery is about deepening my connection to the Universal Source, or Higher Power, or God, or any reference to that Divine Presence that you prefer. It is connection that is important. Ways to do that? Pray for guidance, practice meditation, spend quiet time in nature, be grateful, forgive, and know that all is on time and unfolding as it should. Breathe deeply. Live in the here and now. Let go of judgment and fear. Feel the freedom and peace that is available to you. Accept all.

Spirituality: The Fifth Recovery Commitment

Now we have Level Five. Just what is it we are committing to at this point in the recovery process? We are focused on being completely present, in the now, living fully in this moment, this day. We affirm "Today, I begin a new life". We commit to an "attitude of gratitude", being grateful for everything. We commit to forgiveness, forgiving all. We commit to the flow, the natural course that life is taking. We commit to spiritual practice, prayer and meditation. We commit to acceptance, letting go of the demand that life, or others, be a certain way. We commit to peace of mind and true happiness. Spirit enfolds and holds us.

Spirituality Day:

Breathe deeply. Know in the depths of your being that you are on the right path and that health and wholeness are today's gifts. The light of the Spirit guides and comforts. We are here to be happy and to embrace the wonder of it all. This life is ours to live fully and abundantly. Thank You for all of these blessings. Inner peace and security, right companionship and love, divine purpose, these things are real and present. The miraculous aspect of the recovery process is unfolding and uploading. Let it be!

Spirituality: The fifth of the "Big Five" for Recovery

When pondering Spirituality as a recovery value/commitment, we are being "Spiritual". The contemplation, consideration, time to think, just quietly being with it, all of this is Spiritual practice. To ask oneself "What is my purpose?", "Who or What is in control?", "How do I get and maintain close contact with a Higher Power?". All of this mental activity is useful. We will be provided answers and we will be guided. Life will unfold as it should. It is the point of all of this that we will be brought home to peace.

Spirituality Day:

Freedom emerges as a Spiritual principle in recovery. Freedom from active addiction, freedom from traumatic stress, freedom from mental illness; all are our birthright. We become free from worry. We gain freedom from the shackles of the past. Freedom from debilitating symptoms of these conditions allow us to experience life in all its glory and joyous abundance. We are truly blessed with the freedom to live the life we could only imagine when we were looking through the filter of pain and confusion. Surrender to the healing Spirit and be free. Breathe deeply and freely. Clothe yourself in the Light. Peace.

Spirituality: Recovery commitment #5

Surrender. Let go. Accept. Let it be. Turn it over. Get over it. Move on. Be here now. It is in God's hands. It is what it is. Relax. Breathe.

Pray for guidance. Meditate. Be grateful. The Universe supports us.

Nothing and no one is a mistake. All happenings are to our benefit.

All good advice and helpful. Embrace Truth. Be of good cheer....

The point of Spiritual practice is gaining peace of mind, a goal we all share. It is what was missing when addicted, traumatized, or mentally disturbed. Commit to enhancing contact and reliance on a Higher Power. We do become empowered ourselves as a result. Smile.

Spirituality Day:

This is a day to be thankful. Today I am grateful for Sobriety. I give thanks for Love. I am thankful for Unity. Today I give thanks for Growth. I know that Spiritual protection and guidance are mine for the asking. Thankful for all these blessings and more.

Living in the here and now, with an attitude of gratitude, brings peace.

Affirmation: "I am at one with the Power that manifests my desires".

Prayer: "I clothe myself with a robe of light composed of the Love and Power of God, not only for my own protection, but so that all who see it or come into contact with it, are drawn to God and healing".

Spirituality: The Fifth Recovery Commitment

The commitment around Spirituality involves practicing whole-hearted acceptance and letting go of the illusion of control. In recovery, we are free to be ourselves and work on self-improvement, yet we have no control over others and the course that life events take. If we sit in quiet meditation, if we pray for guidance, if we are grateful, we will be carried along on a purposeful path to fulfillment that truly completes us. Living in the here and now, going with the flow of life, allowing for direction from a Higher Power, these are the markers of one in Level Five recovery. This is the experience of peace that we have been seeking all along. Practice makes it happen.

Spirituality: Level Five Recovery

The biggest reward in this recovery process is getting to a place of sustaining peace of mind. The concept of living life "one day at a time" is a crucial element in this regard. It is especially helpful to think in terms of "Each day is a new beginning". These reminders give us a present focus, with the here and now emphasized. The realization that the past is gone and the future is a dream gives us a chance at knowing where true awareness lies. We only have today. That is reality. Be Sober, Safe, Stable. Be Love. Be United. Be Growing, Be Spiritual. Be in recovery. Being in today makes life wonderful.

Spirituality Day

As we practice Spiritual principles in recovery, we learn to trust. We can trust that all is indeed working for our good. These life events that seem negative or hurtful, such as betrayal of trust by another person, turn out to be for our benefit. At the very least, the experiences are lessons. Usually the benefit is around finding ourselves in a better place, with enhanced circumstances. The lesson learned is often to trust the process of life. To trust our intuition. To trust that a Power is operating that guides, instructs, and protects us. We learn to trust over time by remaining in the recovery process and practicing Spiritual principles. Allow life to flow naturally.

Spirituality: The Fifth Recovery Commitment

So, the solution is Sobriety (Safety for trauma, Stability for mental ills), Love, Unity, Growth, and Spirituality. These commitments made and followed bring one to full recovery from any addiction, traumatic stress, and/or mental illness. This solution is a gift. Take it. It is yours.

Be here now. Have an attitude of gratitude. Breathe deeply. Let your light shine. Pray for guidance. Learn to trust your intuition. Peace prevails in a life experience that was once in great turmoil. Revel in it.

Spirituality Day:

To be Spiritual is to be at peace. Peace of mind is the ultimate goal shared by all who have experienced the ravages and severe challenges of addiction, trauma, and/or mental disorders. So, how do we get there? We first get there by being here. Living fully aware in this place, at this moment in time, is a big part of the answer. A daily practice of meditation and prayer brings peace. Daily reading of inspirational articles and books helps. Expressing gratitude and trusting your instincts and intuition helps. Reaching out to assist others in their journey helps. Know that you are in an active partnership with a universal force creating this beautiful life.

Spirituality: The Fifth Recovery Value

Meditation is an important and beneficial spiritual practice. It is simple. It involves sitting quietly, undistracted, focusing attention on an object or on breathing, perhaps counting breathes or feeling the flow of air in and out. The point is to be free from thoughts. Just be. Be still. Take the time each day to have these moments of here and now stillness and peace. Freedom from the thoughts that often serve to disturb is refreshing. We replenish the Spirit in this way. A valuable value to say the least. The final piece of the puzzle of peace.

Spirituality Day:

Having a commitment to Spirituality puts us on a path to healing our separation from the Source. The Power greater than ourselves did not go away. We, through addiction, trauma, and/or mental illness, lost awareness of Its constant presence, the Oneness, if you will.

Those of us in long term recovery (LTR) are truly survivors. Surviving addiction, traumatic stress, and mental ills that have claimed so many other lives, gives us the opportunity to share what has worked.

Sobriety (Safety, Stability), Love, Unity, Growth, and Spirituality is the path to full recovery. Totally grateful for this knowledge. SLUGS for all! All for SLUGS! Pass the word.

Spirituality: Level Five Recovery

This level of recovery involves practicing acceptance of all occurrences in life as part of the plan. We certainly have no control over other people and their decisions any more than we have control over the weather. We learn to respond to even the worst circumstances with clarity and dignity. We understand that living in the now and relaxing into the flow of life is possible and likely as we practice Spiritual principles. Recovery brings peace of mind. This is about expecting nothing and accepting everything. It can be done.

Spirituality: The Fifth of the "Big Five Values" of Recovery

When we reach Level Five in the recovery process, a new perspective has arisen. We no longer seek to control others or the natural order of things. Life takes a more flexible turn. We make plans and set our intentions, we work for our goals, knowing full well that the outcome is not ours to determine. It really is okay to let go completely. This "embracing of the process, releasing of the outcomes" is Spirituality. I am not chairman of the outcomes committee.

Spirituality Day

Once we reach Level Five in the recovery process, we have achieved some semblance of peace. Having gratitude for this life we have been provided, and knowing that Grace has saved us, we move forward in each day with a trust that was not previously possible. This life experience is appreciated as never before. We realize that life is indeed an adventure and the end of the story is yet to be told. We come to the point where it is exciting to think "I am going to stay around and see how all of this turns out". Let it be.

Spirituality: The Fifth Recovery Commitment

Spirituality is ultimately the solution. We learn, through practice, to release control, or the illusion of control. There is a realization that some other force, other than our own will, is the source of peace. So, a commitment to meditation, prayer, inspirational reading, total acceptance, and embracing faith is what we need. When we practice gratitude and follow the guidance presented, we find our way home. This is a matter of surrender. We surrender to win. We stop demanding that life adhere to our selfish desires and accept that the Universe operates for our benefit if we let it. Get out of the way.

Spirituality: The Number Five Recovery Value

As we become more Spiritual in this recovery process, we are more willing to let go of the insistence that other people or life events be a certain way. We are better able to accept that the way things and people are this day, this moment in time, is actually acceptable. We can stop complaining and get on with knowing that all is well. There is a purpose and time for everything. Praying that "Thy will be done" is really the best approach. It is just the way it is. Relax in the awareness that life works perfectly when we let go. Breathe deeply. Be here now and enjoy the ride. This being alive thing is pretty great.

Spirituality Day:

What is "living in the Light of the Spirit"? It involves living fully in the here and now, completely present in the moment. It is about having an attitude of gratitude, being thankful for all that we have been given. It means that through prayer and meditation we find ourselves at peace with the world. We forgive others and we forgive ourselves. An easy smile, spring in our step, a bright view of the future, deep and meaningful friendships, all unfolding as we appreciate life. What recovery has provided cannot be minimized or replaced. Rejoice.

Spirituality: The Fifth Recovery Commitment

The afflictions of addiction, traumatic stress, and mental illness brings a depth
of sickness, loneliness, un-ability, guilt, and shame (lower s.l.u.g.s.) that result
in a spiritual bankruptcy. This means hope is lost and despair reigns supreme.
To fully recover through the process of gaining Sobriety (Safety for trauma,
Stability for mental ills), Love, Unity, Growth, and Spirituality (Higher
S.L.U.G.S.) results in peace of mind and happiness. This is something to
celebrate. Grateful for the Grace that brought us home, we willingly assist
others in discovery of this solution. More Grace and Peace results. Lives are
saved. Quality of life is enhanced.

Spirituality: Fifth Level Recovery

A Spiritual life involves Spiritual practice. We practice by meditating,
praying, reading inspirational material, being kind and forgiving and
compassionate. We practice by being present, living fully in the now.

We appreciate what is available in our natural environment. We are grateful,
practicing an attitude of gratitude. We practice deep breathing, stretching, and
being fully relaxed. Practice makes us more Spiritual. Practice pays dividends.
Repeat daily, routinely.

Spirituality: The Fifth of the "Big Five Values" of Recovery

Through this process of recovery, we learn to have faith, to walk in the light
of the Spirit. Having experienced the ravages and pain of addiction, traumatic
stress, and/or mental disorders, and surviving, we gain strength. With the
experience of Sobriety (Safety for trauma, Stability for mental ills), Love,
Unity, Growth, and Spirituality, we gain awareness. A firm realization that we
are being directed and protected takes hold. The feeling of gratitude envelopes
us. Life is gloriously ours to relish and enjoy.

Spirituality Day

The fifth and final phase of the recovery process, Spirituality, is very much
about transformation. Fear has been transformed into faith. Resistance has
been transformed into acceptance. Judgment has become compassion.
Separation has transformed into community. Ignorance has transformed
into wisdom. Sadness to joy. Shame is conquered. And so it goes. We have
been transformed into healthier, higher functioning, whole beings. We have
come up out of the hell of addiction, traumatic stress, and/or mental illness
into the bright new day of full recovery. This is nothing short of miraculous.

Spirituality: The Fifth Recovery Commitment

As we reach the Fifth Level of recovery, it is apparent that much has changed. There is more peace in our personal world, less conflict and chaos. We find that we are grateful. Faith abounds. We can trust our intuition and instincts. Life seems to work on our behalf. Our relationships have a quality and depth like never before. So, we go on practicing Spirituality with prayer, meditation, reading the inspiring writings available, and breathing deeply as we appreciate the here and now. We fully accept all, respect all, and give back. The Spirit is alive in us and we are walking in Its brilliant Light. Thanks!

Spirituality

The recovering addict needs Spirituality. The recovering trauma survivor needs Spirituality. The recovering mentally ill needs Spirituality. Spirituality serves to bring one to true peace. A deep sense of knowing that our lives are being directed and that the Universe is working on our behalf is the result of Spiritual practice. We just know that these events and circumstances are purposeful and meaningful. These coincidences are synchronicity and Spiritual in nature. Life is a precious gift and is to be celebrated. Onward and upward you wounded one. No more sick, lonely, unable, guilt, and shame (s.l.u.g.s.). Sober (Safe for trauma, Stable for mental ills), Loved/Loving, United, Growing, and Spiritual.(S.L.U.G.S.) now.

Spirituality: Recovery Value Five

Some people struggle with the "spiritual part" of recovery from addiction, traumatic stress, and/or mental disorders. This aspect of a recovery program may seem mysterious or even out of reach for some. Some take a longer time to reach a place of peace and surrender. What is recommended is just showing up for the process. It will come. Staying Sober (Safe for trauma, Stable for mental ills), focusing on Love, Unity, and Growth, will bring you home. Prayer and meditation are fruitful practices. Being in the process is the solution.

Spirituality Day

The ultimate goal in recovery is peace-of-mind. All of the turmoil, confusion, and fear that comes with addiction, traumatic stress, and mental disorders can be lifted through this process. Yes, it requires faith, belief in a Power greater than our selves. Gratitude also serves to bring us to a place of peace. So, living in the light of the Spirit, fully present, in the now, and keeping the faith, is what works. You and I were not brought this far to fail. The "Big Five Values" of Recovery are a gift that keeps giving. Accept and embrace them as your own.

Chapter Six

To Family and Friends

It is so very important to know and understand that your loved one is sick, lonely, unable-to-change, guilt-ridden, and shame filled. If they could do better, they would do better. They need treatment. Good, focused professional care is required for these afflictions. Your first job is this knowledge. You also must love them in a clear, demonstrative way. And it is very important that you insist that their treatment be focused on "The Big Five" values of recovery. It is also very important that you participate in their treatment and offer consistent ongoing support in their recovery efforts.

This stuff is not easy. You will be challenged to detach emotionally, work on yourself, and stay the course in clarity and love. Your own support system is essential. Support groups such as Al-Anon are so very helpful in this regard. They have much to offer around acceptance, understanding, and specific methods for coping and thriving in these situations. Work your own program of recovery. Getting therapy, having your own personal spiritual practice of prayer, meditation, inspirational reading, and time spent in nature are all helpful in this regard. If in Al-Anon, or another 12 Step group, actually working those steps can be a tremendous asset for your personal growth and well-being. The rewards are tremendous. To witness the benefits of long-term, full recovery from any or all of these afflictions is a great, uplifting life experience. It is happening every day, everywhere, and it can happen in the life of your loved one. Stay the course. The miracle of recovery is something not to be missed. You can allow for this to take place in your life. It is truly worth every minute spent doing the work. May you embark on this path and reap all the joy.

To Treatment Providers

I feel such a deep sense of connection to you, my brothers and sisters working in this noble profession. I know full well the challenges you face day in and day out around these difficult to treat afflictions. These work environments are so highly charged with negative emotions and human suffering, that just holding up to the barrage of it all is enough to cause doubt about your choice of careers. Yet, the upside of great reward in terms of witnessing complete transformation in the recovery process is something that keeps you in the game, coming back each day for more.

I commend you and honor you for doing God's work. This effort is nothing short of life saving and clearly quality-of-life enhancing. Give yourself credit for your efforts and knowledge. Know that you make a difference. Embrace the process and release the outcomes. Support your fellow team members and love the afflicted ones. Keep on keeping on, never giving in to discouragement or loss of hope for anyone. Be an enthusiastic advocate for recovery each day. Grow yourself. Know that the problem is brain-based/physical/psychological, and the solution is spiritual. Do not take anything personally while always doing your best each day. Believe!

Have clarity and focus. I remember when seeing an orthopedic specialist following a leg injury, I was told that RICE would be the best treatment. So, Rest, Ice, Compression, and Elevation is what worked. All working in that field agreed on this path. They all were on the same page.

Can we do the same? Sobriety/Stability/Safety, Love, Unity, Growth, and Spirituality (SLUGS) is the best treatment for addiction, mental illness, and PTSD. Let's get on the same page.

Note: I have addressed three afflictions together due to their common co-occurrence. It is essential that when we see any one of these, we also look for the presence of a second or third diagnosis. So many who are addicted also suffer from PTSD and/or mental illness. There is a great amount of commonality and cross-over with these disorders. Treatment can and should be designed for this consideration.

For Prevention

Prevention efforts need to focus on the truth. These afflictions are truly illnesses of the brain, a part of the body. No judgment allowed. The truth around which drugs are most addictive, who is more susceptible to these afflictions, and the real life impact that occurs are topics worthy of focused discussion. Family-of-origin, heredity and trauma, all need attention. Adverse childhood experiences (ACE) need to be included as considerations for causation and those impacted need to be identified as high risk and helped accordingly. Most young people will not be fooled by some of the messages we have provided in the past. Be honest. For example, the truth about opiate drugs is that they are highly addictive, much more so than many of the others. The message should be "it is so good, don't even try it once". Give information about the vast and rising numbers of overdose deaths. Tell the truth about how some illegal, "street" drugs like marijuana and magic mushrooms are not so addictive, nor do they have much mortality associated, and have shown to benefit certain medical/psychiatric/addiction type conditions.

In Summary

We have to do better. The death rate for these afflictions has been on a steady increase for years. Knowledge and action must have clarity and focus. We need a firm foundation for our field and our efforts around caring for those with these afflictions. We need to know, understand, accept, embrace, and love the addicted, the mentally ill, and the traumatized in order to provide the highest level of care.

If you have one or more of these afflictions, get quality professional care, insisting on focused treatment that emphasizes complete recovery. Believe that you can experience total healing and gain long-term recovery. Life can become amazingly fulfilling and so beautiful. You can and will ascend to your highest functioning, realizing your life potential and purpose. Peace of mind is a goal that we all share. Recovery will deliver. Go for it. It is so worth it.

About the author

John Baldasare has a Bachelors in Sociology and a Masters in Mental Health Counseling from Wright State University in Dayton, Ohio and has worked as a therapist, manager, and executive director in addictions, mental health, and trauma programs for over 40 years. He has directed treatment services in Ohio, Arizona, Virginia, and South Carolina. His website is www.FatherJohnBaldy.com, with Facebook pages "SLUGSociety" and "Dayton Model of Recovery". He currently provides consultation and training services, as well as public speaking.

Made in the USA
Monee, IL
27 July 2023

39935861R20056